M000009265

ABOUT THE AUTHOR

Tin Can Magic is written by Captain Sally. She is a boater who provisions for 6 months at a time and only buys onions, cheeses, and eggs during that time period when traveling outside of the states. Her recipes are also relevant for campers, people who travel in recreational vehicles, and those who like the convenience and the economy of not having to go to the grocery often.

Her recipes were developed to take advantage of buying in bulk for the best prices, convenience of storage, and saving time when preparing meals, be it on land or on the water. She and her husband, Carl, have logged over 30,000 waterway miles. They have also boat camped with their ski clubs, and traveled in a travel trailer.

Small spaces are a problem when provisioning for the long haul and also when preparing meals. Her recipes have been developed keeping this in mind. They are practical, easy, and delicious.

WHY THE RECIPES WERE CHOSEN FOR THIS BOOK

For over 32 years, I have spent a great deal of my time in recreational vehicles of one type or another. I have constantly been developing recipes and ways to cope with no refrigeration, with minimal refrigeration, limited storage, and sometimes less than optimum conditions in which to prepare meals. I have done a lot of experimenting using canned foods of all types. Some of these have turned out to be really good products. Some of them will not grace my pantry shelves.

Many different types of canned meats are readily available at your local grocery. They come in a variety of forms from canned to pouches to freeze dried to vacuum sealed. Here is a list of the meats used in this cookbook and why they were chosen:

1) **CHICKEN**: I use both pouches and cans of chicken breast. The pouches are more costly but have the advantage of being in chunks which is preferred in some dishes. The pouches of chicken also taste slightly better. The cans of chicken breast are more economical and extremely versatile. In a lot of the chicken recipes I have added a touch of lemon juice to help make the canned chicken breast taste more like fresh. Both the cans and the pouches of chicken breast are readily available in most markets.

2) **SEAFOOD**: I use both pouches and cans of various seafood. Again, the pouches are more costly but have a firmer texture. The pouches of seafood also taste slightly better. Tuna, salmon, and crab come in

pouches and are usually available in most markets. So far, I have not found shrimp, oysters, or clams in anything but cans. Especially with the canned shrimp, a little lemon juice perks up the flavor and takes away the canned taste.

3) *HAM*: Canned ham is readily available and the flavor has improved tremendously in the last few years. It has turned into a very versatile pantry item making everything from breakfast ham to meatballs and meatloaf. It comes in different sizes of cans; the most common sizes found are from 6 ounces to 16 ounces.

4) *COUNTRY HAM*: This is a cured, commercially vacuum sealed product which has a lot of flavor and uses. If you are a Southerner, you are already familiar with this product. If not, Broadbent Farms. Com is a good source. It comes in whole hams but I really suggest the vacuum sealed, non refrigerated packages of a few ham slices or even chopped pieces of ham.

5) *PEPPERONI*: Pepperoni is familiar to all of us as a topping for our pizzas but it can be used in many other ways. It is sold in sticks but the sticks seem to contain a lot of fat and grease. It is also sold in most markets in non refrigerated vacuum sealed packages of between 2 and 8 ounces.

6) *SUMMER SAUSAGE*: This product is familiar to all of us from meat and cheese trays at parties. However, if handled right, summer sausage is very good when used in other ways.

7) *ROAST BEEF AND GRAVY*: Canned roast beef is found in the canned meat section of nearly every market. It comes in many different can sizes depending on the store brands. Most stores will carry 8 ounce cans. A good source to order canned roast beef is Brinkman Farms.Com. They carry it in both 16 oz and 26 oz cans.

8) *ROAST PORK AND GRAVY*: Wonderful! This is not readily available in most markets but is fabulous. It is available at Brinkman Farms.Com. They carry it in both 16 and 26 oz cans. A 26 oz can furnishes us with entrees on 2 nights and with lunch the next day.

9) *PRECOOKED BACON SLICES*: This is really a time saver and it also adds to your breakfast menus. It is extremely versatile other than just being used for breakfast. I buy it at bulk stores in packages of 72 slices but it is also available (at much higher prices) at most markets. Precooked bacon keeps, at least to its expiration date, at room temperature. After it is opened it does need to be refrigerated so, depending on your usage, the smaller sized packages might be desirable.

10) *CHEESES*: Cheddar cheese has been used in many of the recipes in this book. Depending on your country if you are outside of the states, you might have to substitute other types of cheese. Cheddar cheese is readily available at good prices throughout the Caribbean islands. I have found that it stores for only a few days when not refrigerated so I buy it in small amounts. Canned cheeses are also available

and are fairly good. They can be ordered online. Processed cheese food is also able to be stored at room temperature. I buy the smaller sizes. Dried cheeses, such as Parmesan, store at room temperature and are quite versatile and tasty.

11) *ONIONS*: Onions are readily available. They store well and perk up the taste of recipes. Dehydrated onion flakes are good and can be added to recipes and can also be re-hydrated with water before using. Onion powder is also a good substitute.

12) *PRODUCE*: These recipes do not use fresh produce except for onions. Some produce stores extremely well. Spaghetti squash, potatoes, sweet potatoes, apples, and citrus fruits are good examples. One of the reasons for not including produce is that it is not readily available in out of the way places. Also, most areas prohibit you from transporting fresh produce from state to state and especially from country to country. However, if it is available I will happily buy and use it.

13) *EGGS*: Eggs are usually available but I will buy 3 dozen at a time and keep them for up to 6 weeks. The trick is to rotate the eggs every 2 days so the yolks stay suspended. They store at room temperature if you do this. I will break the eggs individually into a small bowl before adding them to other ingredients. Another trick is to put the eggs into a bowl of water. If they float they need to be discarded. So far, I have had fewer than a dozen eggs kept this way to spoil.

14) *BUTTER*: Fresh butter is readily available in the Caribbean but may not be available in other areas. Canned butter has the same taste and can be found online through several sources.

METHODS

Often the methods you employ in your galley or kitchen can really be time and energy savers for you. These are some of the methods I use to have more play time:

1) *SLOW COOKER*: I make room for at least a 2 ½ quart and a 3 ½ quart slow cooker. The smaller one is handy for vegetables and the larger one is great for soups and stews. As a USCG licensed captain I often have to plan a boat move on a boat that has no galley equipment aboard. My small slow cooker always makes the trip with us. When traveling, we are not usually plugged into shore electricity and do not like to run the generator for electricity unless necessary. For the slow cooker, a 450 watt inverter, such as the ones sold to recharge your computer battery in the car, will plug into a 12 volt cigarette lighter and will operate the small, older slow cookers on low heat. It is wonderful to have the entire day to play and have your dinner waiting for you.

2) *CASSEROLES AND ONE DISH MEALS*: Many of these recipes are for casseroles and one dish meals. The galley slave needs recipes which are quick, easy, and tasty to keep her/him happy. We can

all cook but there are usually so many interesting things going on around us that we do not want to spend all of our time in the galley. The size of most of these meals is for 2 people. Some are sized for extra company and some can provide planned left overs.

3) *STOVE/OVEN*: Some recreational vehicles do not have ovens. If this is your case, most of the recipes may be adapted easily to stovetop cooking or to slow cooker cooking.

4) *SAVING WATER*: Sometimes water is a major consideration when cooking. We have been in places where water is sold for 45 to 60 cents per gallon. The bottom line is to use as little water as possible but still maintain a good standard of living. Little changes made in the galley make a tremendous amount of difference in water usage.

I mix everything that I can in plastic bags with zippered tops. This works extremely well when mixing things such as muffins and quick breads. When mixed, simply cut a small amount of one corner of the bag off and squeeze the mixture into the pans. Paper cupcake liners for muffins and cupcakes are a great idea. The muffin pan stays clean. The aluminum kind can be used on a baking sheet and do not even require a muffin pan.

Cooking spray is a wonderful item for saving water. Foods do not stick to the pans and clean up is much easier.

Aluminum foil can be used to cover baking sheets when baking various recipes. The baking sheet stays clean under the foil. It is also useful to cover the baking sheet underneath pies and casserole dishes so that any drips are contained on the foil and not on the pan. Aluminum foil can also be used to wrap foods to be put in the oven or on the grill.

5) *PREPLANNED MENUS*: I have chosen to provision for 6 month periods of time when we travel outside of the states. One of the reasons to make this choice was consistency in the quality of foods. Another reason is the economic benefits in buying in bulk and also in taking advantage of sales.

Long term provisioning can easily become a nightmare if you do not have a plan before beginning. I use a very loosely rotating menu for a 21 day period. There are 180 days in a six month period so I multiply this original menu 8 times. This makes it doable. Some days I want to play more and cook less so I keep a laminated menu on a cabinet door and mark off the selections I have already used during that 21 day time frame. This way, every 21 days we have a new rotation of food. Some of you might find it more convenient to plan a 10 day or a 15 day rotation. It is better not to use a 7 day, or a 14 day rotation. By not using a 7 day rotation it prevents the *"This is Thursday so it is spaghetti"* monotony.

Choose foods and recipes that you like and that your crew will readily eat. For instance, if your traveling companion absolutely hates beets it is not a good idea to have them as a main part of the menu 5 of the 21 days. However, it is also good to cater to certain food preferences in order to provide variety. I do not like canned spinach as a vegetable but my husband loves it. Often I will put it on the menu for him and I might put lima beans on the menu for me since he has never met a lima bean he loves. This individualizes the menus somewhat without being hard to do.

I will use close to but not always the same dishes. For instance, if there is chicken vegetable soup on the menu, this could use the same ingredients and become a chicken casserole or chicken patties served with the vegetables which would have gone into the soup. Variety and versatility are very important when choosing your menus.

Using the 21 day loosely rotating menu also gives you a base line for knowing how many of each item to stock. For instance during that time period you might need a can of sliced mushrooms for soup, 2 cans for casseroles, and one can each for an omelet, stew, and a pizza. Count the number of cans of sliced mushrooms needed during that menu rotation, in this case, 6 cans, and multiply that number by the number of rotations you are planning for. By doing this, you can still have the freedom of choice but you will have what you need for that period of time.

6) *SUBSTITUTIONS*: No recipe should be locked in stone! If you are running low on green beans, for instance, you might be able to substitute another item. Often the results are even better than the original idea.

HOW TO STORE ALL THE PROVISIONS

Be creative in your storage solutions. Here are some things that have worked for me:

1) *UTILIZE ALL YOUR STORAGE OPTIONS.* On one boat, there were nice wooden doors covering large openings, Unfortunately these areas were only 4" wide and nearly 24" high with no way to stack anything without having an avalanche when the doors were opened. We made U-shaped wooden brackets that were glued to the inside framework of the storage areas. Removable wood slats were cut to fit these brackets. Now, cans of food could be stacked 4 cans deep. The slats were put in after the cans were added and no more avalanches.

2) *THINK CONSERVATIVELY.* How can I reduce the amount of space these items need? A good example is boxes of diet gelatin. Open the boxes and put 4 packets of the gelatin into one box, you have just saved 3 boxes worth of space. Another way is to group like items. Open all the boxes of lime gelatin and put all those inner packages into one plastic storage container that you mark with the contents. You have saved tons of storage space but you can still know that container has lime gelatin.

3) *SUBSTITUTE.* Canned chicken or beef broth is very handy to use but requires lots of storage space. You have water. Now buy bouillon cubes, bouillon granules, or chicken and beef base. You use almost no storage space and can still have the broth. Prepared salad dressings and gravies are other examples. Consider stocking the dry mixes and making it as needed instead of the bottles of dressing and the cans of gravy.

4) *SUBSTITUTE EVEN MORE.* Fresh milk needs to be refrigerated. A good substitute is boxes of irradiated milk but they are very bulky to store. Nido is dry milk that tastes like milk and can be mixed as you need it. In the Mexican section of your market you will find canned cream. This is a good product and tastes like heavy cream. Canned butter is a substitute when you cannot find fresh butter.

5) *CONSIDER UTILIZING AREAS IN DIFFERENT WAYS THAN THOSE INTENDED.* For instance, snack items such as corn chips, can be difficult to impossible to find in some areas when you are traveling. If you find them, the price can be quite high. I buy what I can conveniently store. Then I put a wood rod across the top of an unused shower. Wire coat hangers can go through the holes in the tops of the bag that were made to hang them in the stores. These coat hangers then hang on the rod and store our corn chips out of the way and so they will not get crushed.

6) *INVESTIGATE YOUR STORAGE AREAS.* Often storage areas may be slightly damp or may have odors that could transfer to products stored there such as paper towels. My husband says that I am the queen of ziplocks! Put the paper towels into the 2 gallon size zippered bags and utilize this space even if it does smell.

7) *USE EVERY INCH OF SPACE.* It is a challenge to utilize every storage option without cutting into your living space and still keeping your living space looking good. My husband likes to drink 1 beer a day. We each like to drink 1 soft drink a day. This equals 14 cases of soft drinks and 7 cases of beer for those 180 days we have talked about. That is a lot of space! No problem. We simply lifted up a mattress on an unused berth and, by using both 24 can and 12 can units, put the drinks under the mattress. The comforter was then pulled down over the extra mattress height and no one knew our hiding place. Of course, about half way through the trip it did become obvious.

8) *CONSIDER EVEN MORE SUBSTITUTIONS.* Crystal Light or any of the other dry drink mixes can be considered for the soft drinks. What items can have a good, smaller substitution? Some things such as the soft drinks you just have to work out for yourselves.

9) *A LOT OF STORAGE SPACE IS REALLY WASTED AREAS.* An example is a hanging locker that can only accommodate 6 hangers with clothes. Adding shelves can open up an area and make it useful.

10) *MAKE STORAGE SPACES ACCESSIBLE.* On boats, as in houses and campers, a lot of storage space is not readily accessible. If this is truly dead space, consider adding a hatch opening and claiming

the space. On one boat, underneath the galley table, we found a space that, when opened up, would store 350 cans of food. A rubber backed throw rug nicely hid the access hatch. Also, examine under settees and under beds for unused spaces.

11) *YOU CAN DECORATE FOR THE HOLIDAYS.* It is still possible to store special items to help you decorate for the holidays and special occasions that are important to you without wasting storage space. Consider collecting plastic place mats for these occasions. Simply lift up a cushion and store the place mats underneath it.

APPETIZERS

Bean and Bacon Dip

BBQ Chicken in Cornbread Cups

Cheese Fondue

Chicken Nests

Crab Nests

Devilled Eggs

Fried Onion Rings

Ham Bites

Ham Nests

Hot Artichoke Dip

Marinated Cheese Cubes

Marinated Mushrooms

Mini Ham Quiches

Pickled Eggs and Beets

Pineapple Salsa

Rosy Pickled Eggs

Shrimp and Pineapple Appetizers

Spiced Pecans

Spiced Walnuts

Stuffed Pickles

Taco Dip

Texas Caviar

Tuna Curry

Very Cheesy Chili Dip

BEAN AND BACON DIP

10 slices precooked bacon, divided
1 4.5 oz can chopped green chilies, drained
1 can black beans, rinsed and drained
1 cup grated Cheddar cheese

1 16 oz can refried beans
1 cup canned corn, drained
1 16 oz can salsa

Set 2 slices of bacon aside for garnish. Chop the remaining bacon. Spray an 8" baking dish with cooking spray. Mix the refried beans, chilies, corn, black beans, and salsa. Spoon into the baking dish. Sprinkle with the grated cheese and top with the remaining 2 slices of bacon which have been chopped. Microwave for 10 minutes. (This recipe may also be baked at 350 for 20 minutes until bubbly.) It may also be made in your crock pot on Low for 2 hours.) Serve with snack crackers, tortilla chips, or small corn cakes (see Breads).

BBQ CHICKEN IN CORNBREAD CUPS

1 tablespoon butter
¼ cup finely chopped onion
½ cup prepared BBQ sauce

1/2 teaspoon garlic powder
2 13 oz cans chicken breast
1/3 cup water if sauce is thick

Sauté the onion in the butter for 3 minutes. Stir in the chicken, garlic, and BBQ sauce. Cook over low heat for 10 minutes, stirring frequently.

Spoon approximately 1 tablespoon of the chicken mixture into cornbread cups (See Bread).

CHEESE FONDUE

8 oz processed cheese spread
2 tablespoons butter
½ cup salsa
Cubes of bread or cornbread
Cubes of summer sausage

2 tablespoons flour
1 cup beer or chicken broth
Small rod pretzels
Cubes of canned ham

Melt the butter and whisk in the flour until mixture is smooth. Stir in the beer and whisk until the mixture just comes to a boil. Simmer for 5 minutes. Cube the cheese and stir into the mixture. Stir until the cheese is melted. Stir in the salsa.

To serve, spear the cubes of bread or meat with a pretzel stick and dip into the fondue. (This is a fun way to serve a fondue and also prevents double dipping.)

CHICKEN NESTS

6 flour tortillas for shells
¼ cup finely diced onion
½ cup black beans, rinsed and drained
½ teaspoon garlic powder
2 tablespoons salsa or taco sauce

1 13 oz can chicken breast
1/2 cup mayonnaise
½ teaspoon cumin
salt, pepper to taste

See Breads for making the tortillas into mini shells.

Mix the drained chicken breast, onion, mayonnaise, seasonings, and black beans. Remove the tortilla shells from the pan and fill just before serving. The filling may be made ahead and refrigerated until use.

CRAB NESTS

6 flour tortillas for shells
1 12 oz can crab, well drained
1/3 mayonnaise
1/8 teaspoon hot sauce

¼ cup finely diced onion
1 teaspoon lime juice
salt, pepper to taste

See Breads for making the tortillas into mini shells.

Mix the crab, mayonnaise, lime juice, and spices. Use the mixture to fill mini tortilla shells. Fill just before serving. The filling may be made ahead and refrigerated until use.

DEVILLED EGGS

6 hard boiled eggs

1 tablespoon spicy mustard

4 to 5 tablespoons mayonnaise

salt, pepper to taste

Shell the hard boiled eggs and slice in half lengthwise. Remove the egg yolks and mash well. Mix with the remaining ingredients until very smooth and creamy. Divide mixture among the egg white halves.

NOTE: Hard Boiled eggs will peel much easier if they are at least one week old.

NOTE: To fill the egg whites, you may use a teaspoon or may choose to put the mixture into a quart zip lock bag and cut a small hole in one corner in order to pipe the mixture into the egg shells.

FRIED ONION RINGS

1 ½ cups all purpose flour

½ teaspoon salt

Vegetable oil for frying

1 12 oz can beer (not light)

2 large onions, sliced ¼" thick

Mix the flour, salt, and beer. Cover and let it stand at room temperature for 1 ½ hour. Separate the onions into rings. Dip the onion rings into the batter and fry a few at a time in the hot oil until golden brown. Drain on paper towels and sprinkle with additional salt if desired.

HAM BITES

1 cup canned ham

2 beaten eggs

¼ cup finely chopped onion

1 tablespoon hearty mustard

Sweet Mustard Sauce

1 cup dry bread crumbs

½ cup grated Cheddar cheese

2 tablespoons brown sugar

Vegetable oil for frying

Flake or mash the canned ham. Mix ½ cup of the dry bread crumbs, the ham, cheese, onion, eggs, brown sugar, and mustard. Shape the ham balls into 1" rounds and roll in the remaining bread crumbs. Press the crumbs into the balls. Refrigerate for 2 hours until firmed up.

Fry the ham balls in at least 3" of hot vegetable oil for 2 minutes until browned. Drain and serve immediately with the Sweet Mustard Sauce (See Sauces and Dressings.)

NOTE: Ground country ham (cured ham which has been sliced and commercially vacuum sealed and may be stored at room temperature) may be substituted for the canned ham.

HAM NESTS

6 flour tortillas for shells
2 cups canned ham
2 diced hard boiled eggs
¼ cup drained pickle relish

½ cup mayonnaise
1 tablespoon mustard
salt, pepper to taste
¼ cup finely chopped onion

See Breads for making the tortillas into shells.

Flake the canned ham with a fork. Mix the ham, mayonnaise, eggs, and spices. Use mixture to fill mini tortilla shells. Fill just before serving. The filling may be made ahead and refrigerated until use.

NOTE: Ground country ham (cured ham which has been sliced and commercially vacuum sealed and may be stored at room temperature) may be substituted for the canned ham.

HOT ARTICHOKE DIP

1 cup mayonnaise
1 can artichoke hearts, drained
¼ cup water chestnuts, drained

½ cup Parmesan cheese
1 4 ½ oz can drained green chilies

Chop the artichoke hearts and the water chestnuts and mix with the other ingredients. Bake at 350 degrees for 15 to 20 minutes.

Serve with thinly sliced bread, snack crackers, or chips. For a more robust appetizer, serve with small fried corn cakes (see Breads).

MARINATED CHEESE CUBES

½ cup olive oil
¼ cup lime juice
½ teaspoon dried basil, crushed
¼ teaspoon garlic powder

½ cup white wine vinegar
1 teaspoon dried parsley
1 teaspoon dried pepper flakes
16 oz Cheddar cheese

Cut the Cheddar cheese into 1" cubes. Combine the remaining ingredients and pour over the cheese. Marinate at least 8 hours. Drain to serve. Serve with toothpicks or small pretzel sticks for easy handling.

NOTE: Prepared Italian salad dressing may be substituted for the olive oil, vinegar, and lime juice.

MARINATED MUSHROOMS

2 8 oz cans whole mushrooms, drained
½ teaspoon garlic powder

½ cup prepared Italian dressing
¼ teaspoon dried basil, crushed

Mix the Italian dressing, garlic powder, and basil. Add the mushrooms to the dressing. Refrigerate and marinate at least 4 hours before serving. These may be marinated up to 2 days.

NOTE: These mushrooms are also delicious when served as a side dish.

MINI HAM QUICHES

¾ cup canned ham, flaked
1 4 oz can chopped ripe olives, drained
¼ cup melted butter
1 cup milk, mixed from powdered
2 tablespoons grated Parmesan cheese

½ cup grated Cheddar cheese
3 eggs, beaten
3 drops hot sauce
½ cup biscuit/baking mix
½ teaspoon ground mustard

Combine the ham, cheese, and olives.
Divide among 12 muffin cups that have been coated with cooking spray.

Mix the remaining ingredients just until blended. Pour over the ham mixture. Bake at 350 for 25 to 30 minutes until a knife inserted near the center comes out clean. Let stand 5 minutes before serving.

NOTE: Ground country ham (cured ham which has been sliced and commercially vacuum sealed and may be stored at room temperature) may be substituted for the canned ham.

NOTE: The canned ham may be replaced with canned chicken breast, precooked bacon, or canned crab meat.

NOTE: To make a richer quiche, substitute ½ cup canned cream and ½ cup water for the milk.

PICKLED EGGS AND BEETS

1 can sliced beets   ½ cup sugar
¼ cup vinegar   ½ cinnamon stick
8 hard boiled eggs

Drain the beets and reserve the juice. Add enough water to the juice to measure ¾ cup. Put the juice, sugar, vinegar, and cinnamon stick into a saucepan. Bring to a boil and remove from the heat.

Put the whole peeled eggs into a plastic container, top with the beet slices. Pour the liquid over and refrigerate at least 4 hours before serving.

PINEAPPLE SALSA

1 cup pineapple tidbits, drained   ½ cup salsa

Mix together. Serve with tortilla chips for dipping. Also good when served over ham.

ROSY PICKLED EGGS

12 hard boiled eggs, peeled   4 cups water
1 cup beet juice, from canned beets   1 cup vinegar
1 small onion, thinly sliced   ½ teaspoon garlic powder
1 bay leaf   2 teaspoons pickling spices
½ teaspoon salt

Peel the eggs and place loosely in a jar.

Combine the remaining ingredients in a sauce pan. Place over low heat until thoroughly heated. Remove the onion. Pour the hot mixture over the eggs. Seal and refrigerate 2 days before serving. Store in refrigerator up to 2 weeks.

SHRIMP AND PINEAPPLE APPETIZER

1 4 ½ oz can salad shrimp, drained   8 oz can crushed pineapple, drained
¼ cup mayonnaise   2 tablespoons chopped onion
2 teaspoons prepared mustard   1 teaspoon dried parsley flakes
2 tablespoons black olives, drained   1 teaspoon lemon juice

Mix all ingredients and chill before serving. Serve with snack crackers or mini corn cakes (See Bread).

SPICED PECANS

1 pound pecan halves   1 egg white
1 teaspoon cold water   ½ cup sugar or sweetener
¼ teaspoon salt   1 teaspoon ground cinnamon
½ teaspoon vanilla

Beat the egg white and water until frothy. Add the pecans and vanilla and stir to coat. Mix the sugar, salt, and cinnamon in a bowl. Add to the nut mixture and mix well. Bake on a cookie sheet which has been sprayed with cooking spray. (To save clean up, you may line the cookie sheet with aluminum foil and then use the cooking spray.) Bake at 225 for 45 minutes, stirring every 15 minutes. Cool and store in a closed container.

NOTE: For small gifts, put the spiced pecans into plastic glasses. Wrap with plastic wrap and tie with ribbon.

SPICED WALNUTS

2 tablespoons butter, melted   ½ cup sugar or sweetener
1 teaspoon orange flavoring   ½ teaspoon salt
2 cups English walnuts

Combine the butter, sweetener, flavoring, and salt. Mix with the walnuts. Bake on a cookie sheet that has been coated with cooking spray. Bake at 225 for 45 minutes, stirring every 15 minutes. Cool and store in a closed container.

NOTE: For small gifts, put the spiced pecans into plastic glasses. Wrap with plastic wrap and tie with ribbon.

STUFFED PICKLES

1 small jar medium sized gherkins   ½ cup tuna or ham salad

Drain the gherkins and dry them with a paper towel. Slice each pickle in half lengthwise. Hollow out each pickle half, leaving a 1/8" rim. Spoon the prepared tuna or ham salad into each half.

TACO DIP

1 can kidney beans, drained   1 can whole kernel corn, drained
1 can black beans, drained   1 can stewed tomatoes
1 can chopped green chilies, drained   1 envelope taco seasoning mix
½ cup finely chopped onion

Mix all ingredients in a slow cooker, Cook on low for 5 hours or on high for 3 hours. Serve with tortilla chips. This dip makes a nice presentation when served in individual small paper cups for individual personal dips.

NOTE: See Soups for Taco Soup.

TEXAS CAVIAR

2 cans black beans, rinsed and drained   ½ cup olive or canola oil
2 tablespoons lemon juice   3 canned jalapeno slices, finely minced
½ finely chopped onion   1 teaspoon salt
1 teaspoon cumin   1 can tomatoes and green chilies

Drain most of the juice from the tomatoes. Mix all ingredients and chill. Serve with snack crackers, tortilla chips, or small corn cakes (See Bread).

TUNA CURRY

1 6 oz can drained tuna, drained

1 can water chestnuts, drained

¼ cup finely chopped onion

1 teaspoon prepared spicy mustard

½ cup mayonnaise

½ cup grated Cheddar cheese

2 tablespoons pickle relish

1 teaspoon curry powder

Finely chop the water chestnuts. Mix all ingredients and serve with crackers or in mini tortilla shells (See Bread.) This is even better the next day.

VERY CHEESY CHILI DIP

8 oz processed cheese food, cubed

¾ cup canned chili, no beans

Mix the cheese and canned chili and microwave for 4 minutes, stirring after 2 minutes. (This recipe may also be prepared in your crock pot on Low for 2 hours.) Serve with tortilla chips, snack crackers, or small corn cakes (see Breads).

VARIATION: Substitute ½ cup salsa for the canned chili.

BEVERAGES

Chocolate Mocha Mix

Cranberry and Grapefruit Juice

Cranberry Punch

Eggless Eggnog

Hot Chocolate Mix

Hot Spiced "Cider"

Lime Water

Mexican Coffee

Minted Chocolate Mocha Mix

Spiced Tea Mix

Spicy Tomato Juice

White Grape Tea

CHOCOLATE MOCHA MIX

½ cup sugar

¼ cup unsweetened cocoa powder

3 tablespoons instant coffee granules

¼ teaspoon ground cinnamon

Mix all ingredients.

For each cup of Chocolate Mocha:

2 tablespoons of mix

1 cup milk made from dry, heated

CRANBERRY AND GRAPEFRUIT JUICE

1 tub of cranberry flavored sugar free drink mix

2 quarts of water

2 cups canned red grapefruit juice

Prepare the drink mix as directed on the package. Stir in the grapefruit juice. Chill before serving.

CRANBERRY PUNCH

1 tub of cranberry flavored sugar free drink mix

2 quarts of water

2 cans of diet ginger ale or lemon lime soda

¼ teaspoon almond flavoring

Prepare the drink mix as directed on the package. Take 6 cups of this mixture and stir in the almond flavoring. Chill the punch and the ginger ale. When ready to serve, mix the ginger ale into the punch.

EGGLESS EGGNOG

6 cups milk made from dry

1 can sweeten condensed milk

1 3.4 oz package instant vanilla pudding mix

1 tablespoon vanilla

¼ teaspoon cinnamon

½ teaspoon ground nutmeg

Additional nutmeg for garnish

Mix all ingredients and chill. Serve each cup of eggnog with a sprinkle of ground nutmeg

HOT CHOCOLATE MIX

1 cup unsweetened cocoa powder
½ teaspoon salt
Mini marshmallows, optional

3 cups powdered milk
1 ¼ cups sugar or artificial sweetener
small candy canes, optional

Combine the cocoa, powdered milk, salt, and sweetener. For each cup of hot chocolate, use 3 tablespoons of the mix and ¾ cup of boiling water.

NOTE: Buy mugs at a thrift store. Fill small cellophane bags with the hot chocolate mixture. Tie the bags with ribbon and put into the mugs. Write the instructions for making the hot chocolate and tie onto the bags. Include small bags of the mini marshmallows or candy canes with the mix. Give as small gifts or as thank you gifts.

HOT SPICED "CIDER"

1 64 oz can apple juice
1 cup canned orange juice
½ cup brown sugar

2 cinnamon sticks
2 tablespoons lemon juice from bottle

Mix all ingredients and bring to a boil. Reduce the heat and simmer for 10 minutes. Remove the cinnamon sticks and serve hot.

LIME WATER

4 cups water
3 tablespoons lime juice

9 packages artificial sweetener

Mix all ingredients and chill.

MEXICAN COFFEE

3 cups brewed coffee, hot
1 teaspoon unsweetened cocoa powder
¼ teaspoon vanilla flavoring

¼ cup brown sugar
1 teaspoon ground cinnamon

Combine all ingredients and serve hot.

MINTED CHOCOLATE MOCHA MIX

1 ½ cups non dairy creamer, powdered
½ cup unsweetened cocoa powder
½ teaspoon peppermint flavoring

1 cup sugar
¼ teaspoon salt

Combine all ingredients.

For each mug of hot chocolate mocha:
3 tablespoons of mix

1 mug of boiling water

SPICED TEA MIX

1 2 oz jar instant tea
¾ cup sugar or artificial sweetener
1 teaspoon cinnamon

1 9 oz jar orange flavored drink mix
1 teaspoon allspice
½ teaspoon ground cloves

Combine all ingredients. Store in an air tight container. For one cup of hot tea, mix 2 teaspoons of tea mixture into ¾ cup of boiling water. For 1 quart of hot tea, mix ¼ cup of the tea mixture into 1 quart of boiling water.

NOTE: Buy mugs at a thrift store. Fill small cellophane bags with the tea mixture. Tie the bags with ribbon and put into the mugs. Write the instructions for making the hot tea and tie onto the bags. Give as small gifts or thank you gifts.

SPICY TOMATO JUICE

1 48 oz can tomato juice
1 teaspoon garlic salt
1 teaspoon hot sauce

1 tablespoon lemon juice from bottle
2 teaspoons Worcestershire sauce

Combine all ingredients. Chill before serving.

WHITE GRAPE TEA

Instant lemon sweetened tea mix

1 cup white grape juice or white grape drink

3 cups water

2 drops mint flavoring

Using the tea jar as a guide, measure out enough powdered tea to make one quart of tea. Combine with the water, juice, and mint. Chill.

BREADS

Batter Bread

Beer Bread

Cheese Straws

Cheese Wafers

Cheesy Onion Bread

Corn Cakes

Cornbread Cups

Crispy Cheese Crackers

Crispy Tortilla Chips

Dumplings

Easy Corn Cakes

Easy Spoon Rolls

Flour Tortillas

Lime Muffins

Mexican Corn Bread

No Knead Cheese Bread

Oat Batter Bread

Pizza Crust

Potato Bread

Pumpkin Slow Cooker Bread

Quick Cheese and Pepper Bread

Simple White Bread

Stir and Roll Pizza Crust

Tortilla Shells

BATTER BREAD

2 cups milk made from dry

1 teaspoon salt

2 tablespoons vinegar

4 cups self rising flour

Mix the milk and the vinegar. Stir into the flour and salt. Pour into a bread pan which has been coated with cooking spray. Bake at 350 for 1 hour. Let the bread cool before slicing.

NOTE: This is basic batter bread to which you may add additional ingredients, such as 1 teaspoon cinnamon and ½ cup raisins, ¼ cup toasted sunflower seeds, or other ingredients of your choice.

BEER BREAD

3 cups self rising flour

1 12 oz beer (not light)

2 tablespoons sugar

Mix all ingredients and pour into a 9" X 5" bread pan which has been coated with cooking spray. Bake at 350 for 1 hour.

NOTE: Finely chopped pre cooked bacon may be added before baking.

CHEESE STRAWS

½ cup grated Cheddar cheese

½ cup all purpose flour

½ teaspoon salt

2 tablespoons softened butter

½ teaspoon Worcestershire sauce

2 to 4 drops hot sauce

Blend all the ingredients well and roll to a thickness of 1/3" on a floured board. Cut the dough into 4" X ½" straws. Bake on a baking sheet (not greased) at 350 for 15 to 18 minutes until crispy.

CHEESE WAFERS

½ cup butter, softened

1 cup all purpose flour

¼ teaspoon paprika

1 cup shredded Cheddar cheese

¼ to ½ teaspoon ground red pepper

Beat the butter and cheese until well blended. Add the remaining ingredients and beat until blended. Chill the dough for 2 hours.

Shape the dough into an 8" log and chill for at least 8 hours. Cut into ¼" slices. Bake on an ungreased baking sheet at 350 for 15 minutes. Cool and store in an airtight container.

NOTE: The easiest way to cut into slices is to cut a piece of dental floss about 18" long. Put the center of the floss underneath the first place to be cut. Bring the ends of the dental floss up over the dough and cross the pieces of floss. Pull both ends and you will have nearly perfect slices.

CHEESY ONION BREAD

½ cup chopped onion	2 tablespoons butter
1 ½ cups baking mix	1 beaten egg
½ cup milk made from dry	1 cup grated sharp Cheddar cheese
½ teaspoon garlic powder	½ teaspoon dried parsley flakes
½ teaspoon dried basil	½ teaspoon pepper
Additional 2 tablespoons melted butter	

Sauté the onion in the butter for 2 minutes until soft. Mix the onion, baking mix, egg, milk, cheese, and spices just until moistened. Put the dough into a bread pan or into a round cake pan which has been coated with cooking spray. Drizzle with the melted butter. Bake at 350 for 30 to 40 minutes until a toothpick inserted at the center comes out clean.

CORN CAKES

½ cup all purpose flour	2 ½ teaspoons baking powder
1 teaspoon salt	1 ½ cups yellow corn meal
3 tablespoons melted butter	1 beaten egg
¾ cup milk made from dry	Vegetable oil for frying

Mix the dry ingredients. Mix the butter, milk, and egg and stir into the dry ingredients. Pour 1 tablespoon of batter into rounds in a greased skillet or griddle. You may need to add 1 to 2 tablespoons milk or water to further thin the batter to the consistency of pancake batter. Cook each corn cake until the edges are dry and the top is bubbly. Turn and cook until golden brown. Serve warm.

NOTE: These corn cakes may be made larger to serve as bread with main dishes. The small size makes a great base for appetizers.

CORNBREAD CUPS

1 cup all purpose flour

¼ cup plus 2 tablespoons grated Cheddar

¼ teaspoon ground red pepper

1 beaten egg white

½ cup yellow cornmeal

¾ teaspoons garlic salt

¼ cup + 2 tablespoons butter

3 tablespoons ice cold water

Combine the flour, cornmeal, cheese, garlic salt, and red pepper and mix until crumbly. A pastry cutter or 2 kitchen knifes may be used. Add the egg and water and mix until the mixture forms a ball.

Roll the dough into 24 1" balls. Firmly press into mini muffin pans which have been sprayed with a cooking spray. Bake at 450 for 8 minutes until lightly browned. Cool in the pans for 10 minutes before removing from the pans.

CRISPY CHEESE CRACKERS

1 cup butter

2 cups all purpose flour

¼ teaspoon hot sauce

¼ teaspoon salt

3 cups grated sharp Cheddar cheese

2 cups crispy rice cereal

1 teaspoon dried red pepper flakes

Mix all ingredients. Roll into 1 ¼" balls. Place the balls on a baking sheet and flatten them with a glass sprayed with cooking spray. Bake at 350 for 10 to 14 minutes until firm. Cool and serve as a cracker.

CRISPY TORTILLA CHIPS

6 flour tortillas

Chili powder

Non stick cooking spray

Lightly spray the tortillas with the cooking spray and sprinkle with chili powder. Turn the tortillas over and repeat. Cut each tortilla into 8 triangles and put on a baking sheet. Bake at 350 for 8 to 10 minutes until crisp.

DUMPLINGS

1 cup baking mix

¼ teaspoon garlic powder

2/3 cup milk made from mix

1 teaspoon dried parsley flakes

¼ teaspoon onion powder

Mix well. Drop by tablespoons into boiling liquid such as chicken broth, beef stew, or chowders. Cook for 10 minutes, stir very gently, and cook an additional 15 minutes.

NOTE: One pot of soup, stew, beans, etc. and drop-in company? Expand the number of servings by adding dumplings.

EASY CORN CAKES

1 19 to 20 oz package corn bread mix	2 beaten eggs
1 cup milk made from dry	½ teaspoon garlic powder
1 teaspoon dried parsley flakes	1 tablespoon dried onion flakes

Mix the spices into the milk and let set for 5 minutes. Stir in the eggs and pour mixture over the corn bread mix. Blend well. Drop the mixture by tablespoons onto a greased griddle or skillet. Cook on the first side until the edges are dry. Turn and cook to a golden brown.

EASY SPOON ROLLS

1 package yeast	2 cups lukewarm water
¼ cup sugar	¾ cup melted butter
1 egg	4 cups self rising flour

Mix the yeast and water. Add the other ingredients. Mix well and store in the refrigerator until ready to use. Spoon into muffin pans which have been coated with cooking spray. Bake at 425 for 20 minutes.

NOTE: This makes 2 dozen rolls and keeps 1 week in the refrigerator.

FLOUR TORTILLAS

4 cups all purpose flour	2 teaspoons salt
1/8 teaspoon baking powder	2/3 cup solid shortening
1 cup + 3 tablespoons hot water	

Mix the flour, salt, and baking powder. Cut the shortening into this mixture with a pastry cutter or 2 kitchen knives until it resembles coarse corn meal. Stir the water in gradually, mixing well.

Shape the dough into 1 ½" balls. Roll out on a floured surface until very thin, approximately 6" diameter. Cook each tortilla in a hot skillet which has not been greased. Cook for 1½ to 2 minutes per side.

LIME MUFFINS

2 cups all purpose flour

½ teaspoon salt

¼ cup milk made from dry

¼ cup canola or vegetable oil

3 teaspoons baking powder

1 cup sugar

2 eggs, beaten

¼ cup lime juice from bottle

Mix the dry ingredients. Beat the wet ingredients together and stir in the dry ingredients. Stir just until moistened. Line a 12 cup muffin pan with paper liners and fill each ¾ full of the batter. Bake at 350 for 25 to 30 minutes.

MEXICAN CORN BREAD

3 tablespoons oil

1 cup yellow corn meal

¼ teaspoon salt

½ cup milk made from dry

½ cup very finely chopped onion

2 tablespoons canned Jalapeno peppers, drained

1 egg, beaten

½ cup all purpose flour

2 teaspoons baking powder

½ cup grated Cheddar cheese

2 teaspoons dried chives, optional

Mince the peppers. Mix all ingredients well. Pour into a 9" baking dish which has been coated with cooking spray. Bake at 350 for 30 to 35 minutes until lightly browned.

NO KNEAD CHEESE BREAD

½ cup boiling water

1½ teaspoons salt

½ cup evaporated milk

1 package dry yeast

3 ½ cups all purpose flour

¼ cup sugar

3 tablespoons oil

2 eggs, beaten

¼ cup lukewarm water

1 cup grated sharp Cheddar cheese

Combine the boiling water, sugar, salt, and oil. Add the milk. Dissolve the yeast in the lukewarm water and add to the sugar mixture. Stir in the eggs. Beat in half of the flour. Beat in the rest of the flour. Let rise for 1 ½ hours until doubled. Add the cheese. Divide the dough and put into 2 bread pans which have been coated with cooking spray. Let the dough rise for 1 hour until doubled. Bake at 350 for 35 to 40 minutes until a toothpick inserted in the middle comes out clean.

OAT BATTER BREAD

¾ cup boiling water	¼ cup butter
2 ½ tablespoons sugar	1 teaspoon salt
1 package yeast	½ cup very warm water
1 cup oats, uncooked	2 ¾ to 3 ¼ cups all purpose flour
1 egg	½ cup chopped nuts, optional

Mix the boiling water, butter, sugar, and salt. Cool to lukewarm. Dissolve the yeast in the ½ cup warm water. Stir the dissolved yeast, oats, 2 cups flour, eggs, and nuts into the first lukewarm mixture. Mix well and stir in enough of the remaining flour to make a very stiff batter. Place in a greased bowl, cover and let rise 1 to 1 ½ hours until doubled in size. Put the dough into a loaf pan which has been coated with cooking spray. Let rise for 30 to 45 minutes until nearly doubled in size. Bake at 375 for 30 to 35 minutes. Cool at least 1 hour before slicing.

PIZZA CRUST

3 cups all purpose flour	1 package fast acting yeast
2 teaspoons sugar	1 teaspoon salt
1 cup very warm water	2 tablespoons olive or canola oil
1 ½ teaspoons Italian seasoning	

Dissolve the yeast in the warm water. Mix all ingredients. Knead on a floured board for 10 minutes. Cover and let it rest for 20 minutes. Divide into 3 equal portions. Roll each portion out to fit on a pizza pan. Bake at 350 for 8 to 10 minutes until it just begins to lightly brown. Top with your choice of toppings and bake until the toppings are bubbly and the cheese is melted.

POTATO BREAD

½ cup instant potato flakes	½ cup all purpose flour
1 teaspoon baking powder	½ teaspoon salt
½ cup boiling water	2 tablespoons cooking oil for frying

Combine the dry ingredients and add the water, mixing and kneading to form very stiff dough. Let stand for 5 minutes. Knead on a floured board. Divide into 6 equal portions. Pat each portion into a round cake approximately ¼" thick. Fry the cakes in the cooking oil until golden brown.

PUMPKIN SLOW COOKER BREAD

¾ cup brown sugar

2 eggs, beaten

¼ cup milk made from dry

2 teaspoons baking powder

1 teaspoon cinnamon

1/3 cup oil

1 cup canned pumpkin

2 cups all purpose flour

¼ teaspoon baking soda

½ cup chopped nuts, optional

Mix the sugar, oil, pumpkin, and eggs. Mix the flour, soda, baking powder, and cinnamon. Stir the dry ingredients into the pumpkin. Beat for 1 minute. Stir in the chopped nuts. Coat a 3 pound coffee can with a heavy coat of cooking spray. Spoon the batter into the pan and cover with aluminum foil. Put the can into a slow cooker and cook on high for 3 ½ hours. Cool for 10 minutes before removing from the can.

QUICK CHEESE AND PEPPER BREAD

2 cups all purpose flour

1 tablespoon sugar

½ teaspoon baking soda

½ teaspoon black pepper

1 tablespoon vinegar

2 eggs

1 cup grated Cheddar cheese

1 teaspoon baking powder

1 teaspoon salt

1 cup milk made from dry

1/3 melted butter

Mix the milk and vinegar. Stir in the butter and eggs, blending well. Combine the dry ingredients. Stir the liquid ingredients into the dry ingredients, stirring until just moistened. Pour into a loaf pan which has been coated with cooking spray. Bake at 350 for 35 to 45 minutes. Cool 15 minutes before removing from the pan.

SIMPLE WHITE BREAD

2 cups very warm water

4 cups all purpose flour

1 ½ teaspoons salt

1 package yeast

1 tablespoon sugar or honey

Mix the yeast, sugar, and ½ cup of the water until dissolved. Mix all ingredients until smooth. Put into a greased, covered bowl and let rise for 2 to 3 hours. Punch the dough down and divide into 2 pieces. Pat each half of the dough into bread pans which have been coated with cooking spray. Spray the tops of the bread with cooking spray. Bake at 350 for 45 minutes to 1 hour until a toothpick inserted into the center of the loaf comes out clean. This makes 2 small loaves of bread.

STIR AND ROLL PIZZA CRUST

2 cups all purpose flour

1 teaspoon slat

¼ cup + 2 tablespoons canola or vegetable oil

2 teaspoons baking powder

2/3 cup milk made from dry

½ teaspoon Italian seasoning

Stir all ingredients together and stir until the mixture leaves the sides of the bowl. Press the dough into a ball and knead until smooth. Roll the dough on a lightly floured board to fit the pizza pan. Brush the dough with 2 tablespoons oil.

TORTILLA SHELLS

6 flour tortillas

Using a 2" biscuit cutter, cut the tortillas (see Breads) into 4 rounds per tortilla. Press into mini muffin pans which have been sprayed with cooking spray. Bake the tortilla shells at 350 for 8 to 10 minutes until they just start to brown. Remove from the oven and cool.

NOTE: May substitute egg roll wrappers for tortillas.

BREAKFASTS

Applesauce Muffins

Bacon and Eggs

Basic Pancakes

Biscuit Squares

Biscuits

Breakfast Quesadillas

Breakfast Pizza

Breakfast Sausage

Chili Omelet

Cinnamon Rolls

English Muffins

Fruit Swirl Coffeecake

Jelly Muffins

Maple Syrup

Overnight Coffeecake

Pancakes

Quick Coffeecake

Sausage and Egg Sandwich

Sausage and Eggs

Special Scrambled Eggs

Special Cheesy Grits

Tuna Omelet

APPLESAUCE MUFFINS

1 ½ cups oats
¾ teaspoon cinnamon
½ cup milk made from dry
3 tablespoons vegetable or canola oil

1 ¼ cups self rising flour
1 cup canned applesauce
½ cup brown sugar
1 beaten egg white

Combine all ingredients and mix only until the dry ingredients are moistened. Spoon into 12 muffin pans which have been coated with cooking spray. Bake at 350 for 20 to 25 minutes.

Note: Before baking, these muffins may be topped with the following mixture: ¼ cup oats, 1 tablespoon brown sugar, 1/8 teaspoon cinnamon, and 1 tablespoon melted butter.

BACON AND EGGS

For each serving:
2 eggs
¼ teaspoon salt
1/8 teaspoon dried chives
Grated Cheddar cheese, optional

2 teaspoons water
¼ teaspoon pepper
1 teaspoon bacon bits

Whisk the eggs, water, salt, pepper, and chives together. Stir in the bacon bits. Scramble in a skillet that has been coated with cooking spray. Top with grated cheese if desired.

BASIC PANCAKES

1 ½ cups all purpose flour
2 teaspoons baking powder
1 egg
¼ cups milk made from dry

1 teaspoon salt
1 tablespoon sugar
3 tablespoons melted butter or oil

Stir all ingredients just until moistened. Cook on a hot greased griddle or skillet until the edges are dry and the pancakes are bubbly. Turn and cook until golden brown.

NOTE: Self rising flour may be substituted in place of the plain flour, salt, and baking powder.

BISCUIT SQUARES

3 cups baking mix   ¾ cup water
1 cup yellow or butter cake mix

Mix all ingredients and stir until just moistened. Knead 10 times on a floured board. Put the dough into a 9" pan which has been coated with cooking spray. Score the surface of the dough, making nine squares. Bake at 425 for 12 to 14 minutes until golden brown. Break the biscuits apart at the score marks.

BISCUITS

2 cups self rising flour   1/3 cup butter
¾ cup milk made from dry

Cut the butter into the flour using a pastry cutter or two kitchen knives. Add the milk and mix. Put onto a lightly floured board and knead 4 to 5 times. Pat out to desired thickness and cut out. Bake at 350 for 15 to 20 minutes until browned.

NOTE: Biscuits make a great base for breakfast sandwiches such as bacon, egg, and cheese. They also make a good topping for casseroles when dropped onto the surface of the hot casserole and baked until browned.

BREAKFAST QUESADILLAS

2 flour tortillas   ¼ cup chopped onion
1 tablespoon butter   6 slices precooked packaged bacon
¼ cup grated Cheddar cheese   2 eggs, beaten
½ teaspoon salt   ¼ teaspoon pepper
2 tablespoons salsa or taco sauce

Sauté the onion in the butter for 2 minutes until tender. Coarsely chop the bacon and mix with the onion. Divide the mixture among 2 tortillas, covering only one half of each tortilla. Cook each egg as for scrambled eggs, shaping each into a half circle the size of a half tortilla. Put one of the eggs onto each tortilla. Divide the salsa between each tortilla.

Fold each tortilla in half and put into a skillet. Heat each side until very lightly browned. Serve with additional salsa if desired.

BREAKFAST PIZZA

4 slices bread
2 tablespoons milk made from dry
½ teaspoon pepper
½ cup grated Cheddar cheese

3 eggs
½ teaspoon salt
12 slices precooked bacon, chopped

Coat an 8" square baking dish with cooking spray. Put the bread into the baking dish, trimming if necessary to make the bread fit. Sprinkle the chopped bacon evenly over the bread. Beat the eggs, milk, salt, and pepper together. Pour over the bacon. Top with the cheese and bake at 350 for 15 to 20 minutes until set in the middle.

NOTE: Use diced summer sausage instead of the bacon. Fry for 2 minutes and blot off any grease before using it on the breakfast pizza.

BREAKFAST SAUSAGE

Summer sausage

Slice the summer sausage ¼" thick and fry for 1 to 2 minutes for each side, until it begins to lightly brown. Blot off any oil before serving.

CHILI OMELET

1 can chili without beans + 2 tablespoons water
Salt and pepper
½ cup grated Cheddar cheese

3 beaten eggs
1 tablespoon milk made from dry

Coat the skillet with cooking spray. Beat the eggs, milk, salt, and pepper together. Pour into the skillet and cook until set, loosening the edges and letting the uncooked eggs under. Flip if desired to cook the other side.

Mix the chili with the water. Spoon desired amount onto half of the egg base. Sprinkle with the cheese. Fold the egg base in half and serve.

CINNAMON ROLLS

2 cups all purpose flour

1 teaspoon salt

¼ cup sugar

2 eggs, beaten

1 package dry yeast

1 cup milk made from dry

¼ cup shortening

Topping mixture

Combine the flour and the yeast. Heat the milk with the sugar, shortening, and the salt until it is warm (115 degrees). Add to the dry mixture. Add the eggs and beat on low speed of an electric mixer for 1 minute; scrape the bowl and beat for 3 minutes at high speed. Shape into a ball and place in a greased bowl, turn once to coat. Cover and let rise until doubled, about 1 hour. Punch down, divide in half and cover. Let rise for 10 minutes.

Roll each half of the dough into a 12 X 8 rectangle. Brush with ¼ cup melted butter. Sprinkle with the following mixture:

¼ sugar

½ cup finely chopped nuts (optional)

2 teaspoons cinnamon

Roll each half up, beginning at the short end. Use dental floss to cut into 12 slices per roll. Wrap the floss around the roll, bring the ends together, and overlap the ends, then pull. Put the rolls into 2 9" pans which have been coated with cooking spray. Cover and let rise 35 minutes until doubled. Bake at 350 for 18 to 20 minutes. You may want to drizzle with a mixture of powdered sugar and water while the rolls are still warm.

ENGLISH MUFFINS

1 cup warm water

1 teaspoon sugar

¼ cup shortening

Cornmeal

1 package yeast

2 teaspoons salt

3 cups all purpose flour

Sprinkle the yeast over the water and mix in the remaining ingredients. Roll the dough out to a thickness of 1/2"on a lightly floured surface. Cut into 3" circles. Sprinkle both sides of the muffins with cornmeal. Let rise until doubled. Cook on a griddle or in a skillet over medium heat until the muffins are lightly browned on both sides and done in the middle. To serve, split the muffins and toast.

NOTE: These make a good base for breakfast sandwiches such as bacon, egg, and cheese. Toast before using for the sandwich.

FRUIT SWIRL COFFEECAKE

½ cup butter

½ cup vegetable or canola oil

4 eggs

1 can cherry pie filling

1 cup sugar

1 teaspoon vanilla

3 cups all purpose flour

Mix the butter and the sugar. Add the oil, vanilla, eggs, and flour. Mix well and spread 2/3 of dough onto a baking sheet which has been coated with cooking spray. Top with the can of cherry pie filling. Dot the rest of the dough over and bake at 350 for 45 minutes. This may be topped with a glaze made from powdered sugar and water.

JELLY MUFFINS

1/3 cup vegetable or canola oil

¾ cup milk made from dry

2 tablespoons sugar

1 ¾ cups self rising flour

1 egg

Jelly, any flavor

Beat the egg; add the milk, sugar, and oil. Mix in the flour only until moistened. Spray 6 muffin cups with cooking spray. Fill them ½ full. Top each with 1 teaspoon jelly. Cover with the remaining batter. Bake at 350 for 25 minutes.

MAPLE SYRUP

4 cups sugar

2 cups water

1 tablespoon maple flavoring

½ cup brown sugar

1 tablespoon vanilla

Combine the sugars and the water and boil for 1 minute. Add the flavorings and stir. Serve over pancakes.

NOTE: More water may be added to make thinner syrup.

OVERNIGHT COFFEECAKE

2 cups self rising flour

½ cup brown sugar

1 cup sugar

1 teaspoon cinnamon

1 cup milk made from dry
2/3 cup melted butter
Topping

1 tablespoon vinegar
2 eggs

Combine the dry ingredients. Mix the vinegar into the milk. Mix the milk, butter, and eggs. Add to the dry ingredients and mix on medium for 3 minutes. Spoon into a 13 X 9 baking dish.

Combine the following:
½ cup brown sugar
1 teaspoon cinnamon

½ chopped nuts

Sprinkle this mixture over the batter. Cover and refrigerate overnight. Bake at 350 for 30 to 35 minutes.

NOTE: The coffeecake may be baked immediately at 350 for 25 to 30 minutes.

PANCAKES

2 cups baking mix
1 cup milk made from dry
1 tablespoon sugar
½ teaspoon vanilla flavoring

2 tablespoons lemon juice
2 teaspoons baking powder
2 eggs

Stir all ingredients just until moistened. Cook until the edges are dry and the pancakes are bubbly. Turn and cook until golden brown.

QUICK COFFEECAKE

Coffeecake:
2 cups baking mix
2/3 cup milk made from mix

2 tablespoons sugar
1 egg

Streusel:
1/3 cup baking mix
½ teaspoon cinnamon

1/3 cup brown sugar
2 tablespoons melted butter

Combine the coffeecake ingredients and pour into a 9" pan which has been coated with cooking spray. Mix the streusel and sprinkle over the top of the cake. Bake at 350 for 18 to 20 minutes.

SAUSAGE AND EGG SANDWICHES

For each sandwich:

2 to 3 pieces summer sausage

¼ teaspoon salt

1 slice Cheddar cheese

1 egg

¼ teaspoon pepper

1 biscuit or 1 English muffin

Slice the summer sausage ¼" thick and fry for 1 to 2 minutes for each side. Blot off any grease before adding it to the sandwich. Toast the English muffin or heat the biscuit. Put the sausage on one half of the chosen bread. Whisk the egg, salt, and pepper together and scramble in a skillet that has been coated with cooking spray. Shape into a round shape to match the bread. Top the sausage with the egg, then with the cheese slice.

SAUSAGE AND EGGS

For each serving:

1 ¼" thick slice of summer sausage

2 teaspoons water

¼ teaspoon pepper

2 eggs

¼ teaspoon salt

Dice the summer sausage slice and sauté for 1 minute. Whisk the eggs, salt, pepper, and water together and stir into the summer sausage. Scramble.

SPECIAL SCRAMBLED EGGS

¼ cup finely chopped onion

2 slices precooked bacon, finely chopped

½ teaspoon salt

2 tablespoons water or milk made from dry

1 tablespoon butter

4 eggs

¼ teaspoon pepper

Cook the onion in the butter for 2 minutes until soft. Beat the eggs, salt, pepper, and liquid well and pour over the onion mixture. Sprinkle with the chopped bacon. Scramble the eggs and serve.

SPICED CHEESY GRITS

1 cup regular grits

1 teaspoon chicken bouillon granules

4 cups boiling water

1 cup grated Cheddar cheese

1 teaspoon Worcestershire sauce   1 teaspoon garlic powder

2 teaspoons dry taco seasoning mix

Add the grits to the boiling water and chicken bouillon. Cook as directed on the box until the water is absorbed. Stir in the remaining ingredients and cook over very low heat, stirring constantly, until the cheese melts.

TUNA OMELET

¼ cup chopped onion   1 tablespoon butter or oil

1 7 oz can tuna, well drained   ¼ grated Cheddar cheese

2 tablespoons salsa   3 beaten eggs

1 tablespoon milk made from dry   salt, pepper

Sauté the onion in the butter. Remove from the skillet. Coat the skillet with cooking spray. Beat the eggs, milk, salt, and pepper together. Pour into the skillet and cook until set, loosening the edges and letting the uncooked eggs under. Flip if desired to cook the other side.

Mix the cooked onion, tuna, salsa, and cheese together. Sprinkle over the egg base. Fold the egg base in half and serve.

NOTE: Canned salmon may be substituted for the tuna.

CHICKEN

BBQ Chicken

BBQ Chicken Pizza

Cheesy Chicken and Rice

Cheesy Chicken and Stuffing

Chicken A La King

Chicken Alfredo

Chicken and Asparagus

Chicken and Bean Burritos

Chicken and Bean Tortillas

Chicken and Biscuits

Chicken and Cheese Pasta

Chicken and Cheese Salad

Chicken and Dried Beef

Chicken and Noodle Casserole

Chicken and Stuffing

Chicken and Vegetable Bake

Chicken Burritos

Chicken Cacciatore Pasta

Chicken Caliente

Chicken Casserole

Chicken Cassoulet

Chicken Chow Mien

Chicken Cordon Bleu Pizza

Chicken Enchilada Casserole

Chicken Enchilada Quiche

Chicken Enchiladas

Chicken in Mustard Sauce

Chicken Loaf

Chicken Patties

Chicken Pot Pie

Chicken Salad

Chicken Shepherd's Pie

Chicken Spaghetti

Chicken Stacks

Chicken with Cheesy Spaghetti

Chicken with Chow Mein Noodles

Chicken with Mushrooms

Curried Chicken Salad

King Ranch Chicken

Lemon Chicken Chow Mein

Lemon Chicken with Pasta

Peanut Chicken

Spanish Rice with Chicken

Stacked Mexican Chicken

Sweet & Sour Chicken

Teriyaki Chicken with Rice

Thai Chicken

Thai Chicken with Pasta

Tropical Chicken Salad

BBQ CHICKEN

1 13 oz can chicken breast
2 drops smoked hickory flavoring
¼ teaspoon onion powder

½ cup prepared BBQ sauce
¼ teaspoon garlic powder

Mix all ingredients and bring to a boil. Lower the heat and simmer for 5 minutes. Serve on buns with pickle and sliced onions for sandwiches or serve on plates with chopped pickles and chopped onions as topping.

BBQ CHICKEN PIZZA

1 12" pizza crust
¼ teaspoon smoked hickory flavoring
½ cup canned black beans, rinsed and well drained

1/3 cup prepared BBQ sauce
1 13 oz can chicken breast
1 cup grated Cheddar cheese

Bake the pizza crust at 350 for 5 minutes. Spread the BBQ sauce over the crust. Mix the smoke flavoring with the chicken breast and spoon evenly over the crust. Put the black beans over the chicken. Top with the cheese and bake at 350 for 15 minutes until bubbly.

CHEESY CHICKEN AND RICE

1 13 oz can chicken breast
1 cup processed cheese food, grated
1 4 oz can sliced mushrooms, drained
Hot cooked rice

1 can cream of chicken soup
1 teaspoon dried chives
½ cup canned mixed vegetables, drained

Combine the chicken, soup, cheese, chives, mushrooms, and vegetables. Heat to boiling and reduce the heat. Simmer for 5 minutes and serve over the rice.

CHEESY CHICKEN AND STUFFING

1 6 oz package stuffing mix for chicken
1 can cream of chicken soup
1 cup grated cheddar cheese

1 13 oz can chicken breast
1 4 oz can black olives, drained

Prepare the stuffing mix as directed on the package. Combine the stuffing with the remaining ingredients. Pour into a baking dish that has been coated with cooking spray. Bake at 350 for 30 minutes.

CHICKEN A LA KING

¼ cup chopped onion

1 13 oz can chicken breast

½ cup milk made from dry

2 tablespoons diced canned pimientos

4 slices of toasted bread

1 tablespoon oil

1 can cream of chicken soup

1 4 oz can sliced mushrooms, drained

½ teaspoon pepper

Sauté the onion in the oil for 2 minutes until tender. Stir in the chicken, soup, milk, mushrooms, pimientos, and pepper. Bring to the boiling point. Reduce the heat and simmer for 10 minutes. Serve over the toasted bread.

CHICKEN ALFREDO

8 oz spaghetti or linguini

1 can cut green beans, drained

½ cup milk

1 can sliced mushrooms, drained

1 13 oz can chicken breast

1 chicken bouillon cube

1 can cream of mushroom soup

½ cup grated Parmesan cheese

½ teaspoon pepper

Cook the pasta in boiling water with the bouillon cube. Add the green beans during the last 3 minutes of cooking. Drain and keep warm. Mix the remaining ingredients and cook over medium heat for 10 minutes. Add the pasta and cook 5 more minutes.

CHICKEN AND ASPARAGUS

1 13 oz can chicken breast

1 4 oz can sliced mushrooms, drained

2 cups corkscrew pasta, cooked

¾ cup round buttery cracker crumbs

1 can asparagus, drained

1 can cream of chicken soup

¼ cup butter

1 can sliced mushrooms, drained

Cut the asparagus into 1" pieces. Mix the asparagus, chicken, mushrooms, cooked pasta, and soup. Pour into a baking dish that has been coated with cooking spray. Melt the butter and stir into the cracker crumbs. Sprinkle the crumb mixture over the casserole. Bake at 350 for 30 minutes.

CHICKEN AND BEAN BURRITOS

1 13 oz can chicken breast
1 ½ teaspoons chili powder
1 4 oz can chopped green chilies, drained
¼ cup finely chopped onion

1 can black beans, rinsed and drained
1 8 oz can tomato sauce
1 cup grated Cheddar cheese
5 to 6 flour tortillas

Combine the chicken, beans, chili powder, tomato sauce, chilies, cheese, and onion. Divide among the tortillas. Tuck the ends of the tortillas in and roll. Place seam side down in a skillet and cook for 10 minutes, turning them so that they are very lightly browned.

CHICKEN AND BEAN TOSTADAS

4 corn tortillas
1 7 oz can chicken breast
½ teaspoon garlic powder
½ teaspoon cumin
½ cup grated Cheddar cheese

¼ cup oil
1 can black beans, rinsed and drained
½ teaspoon chili powder
1 teaspoon lime juice from bottle
¼ cup prepared salsa or taco sauce

Put the oil into a skillet and fry the corn tortillas one at a time for 2 minutes on each side until crispy. Drain on paper towels. Combine the chicken, beans, spices, and lime juice and divide the mixture over the tostadas. Sprinkle with the cheese. Top each tostada with 1 tablespoon of the salsa.

CHICKEN AND BISCUITS

1 13 oz can chicken breast
1 4 oz can sliced mushrooms, drained
½ cup grated Cheddar cheese

1 can mixed vegetables, drained
1 can cream of chicken soup

Biscuit topping:
1 ½ cups baking mix
½ cup grated Cheddar cheese

2/3 cup milk made from dry

Combine the chicken, vegetables, soup, and cheese. Pour into a baking dish that has been coated with cooking spray. Bake at 350 for 20 minutes until bubbly.

Mix the baking mix and the milk. Drop the batter by tablespoons onto the chicken mixture. Bake uncovered, for 25 minutes until the biscuits are browned. Top with the cheese and bake for 5 more minutes.

CHICKEN AND CHEESE PASTA

3 cups cooked pasta

¼ cup milk made from dry

1 teaspoon chicken bouillon granules

1 7 oz pouch chicken breast

1 can sliced mushrooms, drained

8 oz processed cheese food

1 tablespoon ketchup

1 teaspoon prepared mustard

½ cup cut green beans, drained

Combine the milk and cheese with the bouillon, ketchup, and mustard. Cook on medium heat until the cheese has melted and the mixture is bubbly. Stir in the pasta, peas, mushrooms, and chicken. Cook 5 more minutes, stirring frequently.

CHICKEN AND CHEESE SALAD

1 13 oz can chicken breast

½ teaspoon chicken bouillon granules

½ cup grated Cheddar cheese

½ cup mayonnaise

2 tablespoons finely chopped onion

1 teaspoon dried chives

1 tablespoon lemon juice

¼ cup slivered almonds, toasted

Lightly toast the almonds in a skillet for 2 minutes and let cool. Mix the mayonnaise, lemon juice, and bouillon until the bouillon dissolves. Stir in the other ingredients. This makes a good sandwich spread. It can also be served mounded on a small plate for a light lunch.

CHICKEN AND DRIED BEEF

1 13 oz can chicken breast

1 can cream of chicken soup

1 can canned peas and carrots, drained

1 5 oz jar dried beef

½ cup water

1 package yellow rice mix

Prepare the rice mix as directed on the package. Dice the dried beef. Mix the beef, chicken, soup, water, and vegetables. Bring to a boil. Reduce the heat and simmer for 5 minutes. Serve over the rice.

CHICKEN AND NOODLE CASSEROLE

2 pouches chicken breast

½ cup water or chicken broth

1 can peas with carrots, drained

½ teaspoon Worcestershire sauce

½ cup coarsely broken saltine crackers

1 can cream of chicken soup

1 4 oz can sliced mushrooms, drained

1 teaspoon prepared mustard

2 cups cooked noodles

½ cup grated Cheddar cheese

Mix the chicken, soup, water, mushrooms, peas and carrots, mustard, and Worcestershire sauce. Stir in the noodles and pour into a baking dish which has been coated with cooking spray. Bake at 350 for 30 to 35 minutes until bubbly. Mix the crackers and the cheese and sprinkle over the casserole. Bake an additional 5 minutes.

CHICKEN AND STUFFING

1 13 oz can chicken breast

1 6 oz box cornbread stuffing mix

¼ cup water

1 8 oz can crushed pineapple

Mix the chicken and water and put into the bottom of a baking dish that has been coated with cooking spray. Prepare the stuffing mix as directed on the box, substituting the pineapple juice for part of the liquid. Stir the pineapple into the stuffing. Put the stuffing over the chicken and bake at 350 for 30 minutes.

CHICKEN AND VEGETABLE BAKE

1 13 oz can chicken breast

½ cup grated Cheddar cheese

1½ cups milk made from dry

1 teaspoon paprika

½ teaspoon pepper

1 can mixed vegetables, drained

½ cup baking mix

2 teaspoons spicy mustard

½ teaspoon dried parsley flakes

2 eggs, beaten

Mix the chicken and the vegetables. Beat the remaining ingredients together and combine with the chicken mixture. Pour into a baking dish that has been coated with cooking spray. Bake at 350 for 45 minutes.

CHICKEN BURRITOS

1 13 oz can chicken breast
½ cup salsa
1 cup grated Cheddar cheese
5 to 6 flour tortillas

1 cup cooked rice
1 4½ oz can chopped green chilies, drained
¼ cup finely chopped onion

Combine the chicken, rice, salsa, chilies, cheese, and onion. Divide among the tortillas. Tuck the ends of the tortillas in and roll. Place seam side down in a skillet and cook for 10 minutes, turning them so that they are very lightly browned.

CHICKEN CACCIATORE PASTA

3 cups penne pasta, cooked
1 can sliced mushrooms, drained
1 tablespoon oil
1 teaspoon dried chives
1 14 oz can tomato sauce

1 pouch chicken breast
¼ cup chopped onion
½ teaspoon garlic powder
1 teaspoon Italian seasoning
½ teaspoon pepper

Cook the pasta, drain, and keep warm. Sauté the onion in oil for 2 minutes until tender. Stir in the remaining ingredients and cook on medium heat for 10 minutes, stirring frequently.

CHICKEN CALIENTE

3 cups corn chips
1 13 oz can chicken breast
1 4 ½ oz can chopped green chilies, drained
1 cup grated Cheddar cheese

1 can cream of chicken soup
1/3 cup chopped onion
1 4 oz can sliced black olives, drained

Coarsely crush the corn chips and sprinkle half of the chips into a baking dish that has been coated with cooking spray. Bake 5 minutes at 350 until lightly browned. Blend the soup, chicken, onion, chilies, and olives and pour over the corn chips. Top with the remaining corn chips and bake at 350 for 20 minutes. Top with the cheese and bake an additional 5 minutes.

CHICKEN CASSEROLE

2 pouches chicken breast
1 can mixed vegetables, drained
½ cup grated Cheddar cheese
Pepper to taste

1 can cream of chicken soup
1 can sliced mushrooms, drained
1 teaspoon chicken bouillon granules
French fried onions

Mix all ingredients except the onion rings. Pour into a baking dish which has been coated with cooking spray. Bake at 350 for 30 to 35 minutes until bubbly. Top with the onion rings and bake an additional 5 minutes. Let the casserole rest 10 minutes before serving in order to let it thicken slightly.

NOTE: Cracker crumbs may be used in the place of the onion rings.
NOTE: 13 ounces of chicken breast may be used in the place of the chicken pouches.

CHICKEN CASSOULET

½ cup chopped onion
½ cup canned carrot slices, drained
1/3 cup water
1 teaspoon garlic powder
2 cans navy beans, rinsed and drained

1 tablespoon butter
6 oz tomato paste
½ cup dry red wine or water
2 bay leaves
2 pouches chicken breast

Sauté the onion in the butter for 2 minutes. Mix all ingredients in a slow cooker. Cook on low for 6 to 8 hours or on high for 4 to 6 hours.

CHICKEN CHOW MEIN

1 can golden mushroom soup
1 tablespoon soy sauce
1 teaspoon Worcestershire sauce
½ cup chopped onion
2 pouches chicken breast
1 can Chinese vegetables, drained
Cooked rice

½ cup water
1 beef bouillon cube
½ teaspoon curry powder
½ cup diced canned roasted red pepper
1 4 oz can sliced mushrooms, drained
Chow mein noodles

Mix all ingredients except the noodles and rice. Cook on high in the microwave for 12 minutes, stirring every 2 minutes. Serve over rice that has been topped with Chow mein noodles.

NOTE: A can of mixed vegetables may be substituted for the can of Chinese vegetables.

CHICKEN CORDON BLEU PIZZA

1 12" pizza crust
1 7 oz can chicken breast
¼ cup finely chopped onion
1 cup grated Cheddar cheese

1/3 cup prepared ranch salad dressing
½ cup chopped country ham or canned ham
¼ cup sliced green olives

Bake the pizza crust at 350 for 5 minutes. Spread the ranch dressing over the crust. Top with the remaining ingredients in the order given. Bake at 350 for 15 minutes until bubbly. Let stand for 5 minutes before slicing.

CHICKEN ENCHILADA CASSEROLE

1 can tomato soup
1 13 oz can chicken breast
½ cup grated Cheddar cheese

½ cup salsa
4 8" flour tortillas, cut into strips

Mix the soup, salsa, chicken, and tortilla strips. Pour into a baking dish that has been coated with cooking spray. Top with the cheese and bake at 350 for 25 minutes.

CHICKEN ENCHILADA QUICHE

1 unbaked pie crust
½ cup milk made from dry
1 ½ cups broken tortilla chips
1 cup salsa
Salt, pepper to taste

4 eggs
1 13 oz can chicken breast
1 cup grated Cheddar cheese
1 4 ½ oz can drained green chilies

Fit the pie crust into a 9" pie plate and flute around the edges. Beat the eggs, salt, pepper, and milk. Stir in the chips, chilies, salsa, and cheese. Pour into the pie shell and bake at 350 for 50 to 60 minutes. Serve with additional salsa.

NOTE: Broken saltine crackers would make an acceptable substitute for the tortilla chips. Omit the salt.

CHICKEN ENCHILADAS

1 13 oz can chicken breast
1 4 ½ oz can chopped green chilies, drained
5 to 6 flour tortillas
½ teaspoon garlic powder

½ cup salsa
1 cup grated Cheddar cheese
1 can cream of chicken soup
½ teaspoon onion powder

Combine the chicken, salsa, and green chilies. Divide the mixture among the tortillas and roll up. Put the enchiladas seam side down in a baking dish that has been coated with cooking spray. Mix the soup and the spices and pour over the enchiladas. Bake 20 minutes at 350. Top with the cheese and bake an additional 5 minutes.

CHICKEN IN MUSTARD SAUCE

1 13 oz can chicken breast
1 teaspoon lemon juice from bottle
½ cup water
Hot cooked rice or pasta

2 tablespoons spicy mustard
1 can cream of chicken soup
1 can artichoke hearts, drained

Drain the artichoke hearts and chop. Mix the soup, water, and mustard and heat to a boil. Reduce the heat and stir in the chicken and artichokes. Reduce the heat and simmer for 5 minutes. Serve over the rice or pasta.

CHICKEN LOAF

¼ cup finely diced onion
1 ½ cups chicken flavored dressing mix
2 beaten eggs
2 13 oz cans chicken breast, drained

1 tablespoon butter
1 can cream of chicken soup
½ teaspoon chicken bouillon granules

Sauté the onion in the butter for 2 minutes until tender. Mix all the ingredients and put into a loaf pan which has been sprayed with cooking spray. Bake at 350 for 40 to 50 minutes until set and lightly browned.

NOTE: For ease of removing the loaf, the pan may be lightly sprayed with the cooking spray and then coated with heavy aluminum foil which extends over the edges of the pan. Spray the foil with a heavy coat of the cooking spray.

NOTE: This is great when sliced and topped with the Welch Rarebit Sauce or the Tomato Rarebit Sauce (See Sauces).

CHICKEN PATTIES

½ cup chopped onion
1 13 oz can chicken breast
½ cup saltine cracker crumbs
¼ teaspoon pepper

1 tablespoon butter
½ teaspoon chicken bouillon granules
2 beaten eggs
2 tablespoons oil for frying

Sauté the onion in the butter for 2 minutes until tender. Cool. Mix the onion and the remaining ingredients well. Form into patties. Fry in the oil for 5 minutes per side, until golden brown.

NOTE: These are also great for sandwiches, either hot or cold.
NOTE: Try topping the patties with a hot cheese sauce.

CHICKEN POT PIE

1 cup self rising flour
1 cup milk made from dry
1 can peas and carrots, drained
1 can cream of chicken soup

½ cup melted butter
1 13 oz can chicken breast
1 can whole potatoes, drained

Mix the flour, melted butter, and milk. Dice the potatoes. Mix the potatoes, chicken, carrots, peas, and soup. Pour into a baking dish that has been coated with cooking spray. Pour the flour batter over the chicken mixture. Put the pie plate on a baking tray that has been lined with aluminum foil to catch any drips as the pie bakes. Bake at 350 for 35 to 45 minutes until the top crust is lightly browned.

NOTE: 2 cans of mixed vegetables, drained, may be substituted for the peas, carrots, and potatoes.

CHICKEN SALAD

1 13 oz can chicken breast
¼ cup pickle relish, drained
1 teaspoon chicken bouillon granules

½ cup mayonnaise
¼ cup finely chopped onion

Mix the mayonnaise and the bouillon granules. Stir in the remaining ingredients and mix well. Chill before serving. This may be served as a filling for a sandwich or mounded on small plates as a lunch entrée.

CHICKEN SHEPHERD'S PIE

1 package instant mashed potato flakes
1 can peas and carrots, drained
1 can cream of chicken soup
½ cup grated Cheddar cheese

2 pouches chicken breast
1 4 oz can sliced mushrooms, drained
¼ cup water

Prepare the instant mashed potatoes as directed on the package. Mix all other ingredients together and pour into a baking dish which has been coated with cooking spray. Top with the prepared potatoes, leveling them out evenly over the chicken mixture. Bake at 350 for 30 minutes until the potatoes begin to lightly brown. Sprinkle with the cheese and bake for 5 more minutes.

CHICKEN SPAGHETTI

3 cups cooked spaghetti
1 cup grated Cheddar cheese
1 14 oz jar spaghetti sauce
½ teaspoon onion powder
1 tablespoon grated Parmesan cheese

1 chicken bouillon cube
1 7 oz can chicken breast
½ teaspoon garlic powder
½ teaspoon pepper

Cook the pasta in boiling water with the bouillon cube. Mix the spaghetti sauce with the spices. Mix in the chicken and the pasta. Sprinkle with the Parmesan cheese. Bake at 350 for 25 to 30 minutes until bubbly.

CHICKEN STACKS

1 2 oz can chow mein noodles
1 can chicken gravy
1 can Mandarin oranges, drained
¼ cup sliced almonds

2 cups cooked rice
1 8 oz can pineapple tidbits, drained
¼ cup flaked coconut
1 13 oz can chicken breast

Mix the canned chicken breast with 2 to 3 tablespoons of the gravy and heat. Heat the rest of the gravy separately. Put a tablespoon of the chow mein noodles on each plate. Then, stack in this order: rice, chicken, pineapple, oranges, and coconut.. Top with the gravy.

CHICKEN WITH CHEESY SPAGHETTI

8 oz uncooked spaghetti
1 tablespoon canola or olive oil

1 chicken bouillon cube
1 teaspoon garlic powder

1 teaspoon dried chives
5 slices processed cheese spread
1 13 oz can chicken breast

1 can cream of chicken soup
½ cup water
1 can sliced mushrooms, drained

Cook the spaghetti in boiling water with the bouillon cube. Mix the oil, garlic, and chives together and toss with the hot, drained spaghetti. Mix the soup, cheese slices, and water and cook on medium heat for 5 minutes until the cheese has melted. Stir in the chicken and mushrooms and cook 5 minutes. Stir in the spaghetti and cook until heated through.

CHICKEN WITH CHOW MEIN NOODLES

1 can sliced green beans, drained
1 13 oz can chicken breast
1 8 oz can chow mein noodles

1 can cream of chicken soup
1 4 oz can sliced mushrooms, drained

Mix the green beans, soup, chicken, and mushrooms together and cook over medium heat for 10 minutes. Serve over the chow mein noodles.

CHICKEN WITH MUSHROOMS

1 13 oz can chicken breast
1 8 oz can tomato sauce
¼ teaspoon onion powder
½ teaspoon pepper
Hot cooked rice

1 4 oz can sliced mushrooms, drained
¼ teaspoon garlic powder
1 teaspoon dried chives
¼ cup water

Mix the chicken, mushrooms, sauce, water, and spices. Bring to a boil and reduce the heat. Simmer for 5 minutes. Serve over the rice.

CURRIED CHICKEN SALAD

1 13 oz can chicken breast
¼ cup finely chopped onion
¼ to 1/3 cup mayonnaise

1 teaspoon chicken bouillon granules
1 teaspoon curry powder
¼ cup pickle relish

Mix all ingredients and chill before serving.

KING RANCH CHICKEN

½ cup chopped onion

1 can cream of chicken soup

1 13 oz can chicken breast

1 cup grated Cheddar cheese

1 tablespoon oil

¾ cup salsa

6 corn tortillas

Tear the corn tortillas into bite sized pieces. Sauté the onion in the oil for 2 minutes until tender. Mix the onions, soup, salsa, and chicken. Put 1/3 of the corn tortillas into an 8" baking dish that has been coated with cooking spray. Layer with 1/3 of the chicken mixture and 1/3 cup of the cheese. Repeat the layers 2 more times. Bake at 350 for 30 minutes.

LEMON CHICKEN OVER CHOW MEIN NOODLES

1 13 oz can chicken breast

1 tablespoon lemon juice from bottle

1 teaspoon soy sauce

½ teaspoon garlic powder

1 5 oz can chow mein noodles

½ cup water

1 tablespoon corn starch

1 teaspoon dried chives

1 can mixed vegetables, drained

Mix the water, lemon juice, and corn starch until smooth. Bring to a boil, reduce the heat, and simmer for 5 minutes. Stir in the chicken, soy sauce, spices, and vegetables. Simmer for 5 minutes. Serve over the chow mein noodles.

LEMON CHICKEN WITH PASTA

8 oz corkscrew pasta

½ cup butter

1 teaspoon dried chives

½ teaspoon garlic powder

1 13 oz can chicken breast

1 chicken bouillon cube

2 tablespoons lemon juice

½ teaspoon dried parsley

¼ teaspoon dried basil, crushed

Cook the pasta in boiling water with the bouillon cube as directed on the package. Drain the pasta. Melt the butter and stir in the remaining ingredients. Pour over the pasta and mix. If desired, grated Parmesan cheese may be added to each serving.

PEANUT CHICKEN

1 13 oz can chicken breast
2 teaspoons soy sauce
¼ teaspoon garlic powder
1 can water chestnuts, drained
Peanuts for garnish

¼ cup peanut butter
¾ cup water
1 teaspoon dried chives
Hot cooked rice

Combine the chicken, peanut butter, soy sauce, water, chestnuts, and spices and bring to a boil. Reduce the heat and simmer for 5 minutes. Serve over the rice and sprinkle with peanuts.

SPANISH RICE WITH CHICKEN

2 tablespoons oil
½ cup chopped onion
1 cup of water
½ teaspoon cumin
2 pouches chicken breast

1 cup uncooked rice
2 chicken bouillon cubes
1 cup salsa
½ teaspoon chili powder

Brown the onion and the rice in the oil for 5 minutes. Mix the bouillon cubes and the water and add to the rice. Add the salsa and the spices. Bring to a boil, cover and simmer for 20 minutes until the liquid is absorbed, stirring every 5 minutes. Stir in the chicken breast and heat.

NOTE: One 13 oz can of chicken breast may be used in the place of the chicken pouch.

STACKED MEXICAN CHICKEN

½ cup chopped onion
1 teaspoon garlic powder
1 13 oz can chicken breast
1 can green chilies, drained
1 cup grated Cheddar cheese, divided
6 flour tortillas

1 tablespoon oil
1 16 oz can stewed tomatoes
8 oz can tomato sauce
1 teaspoon cumin
¼ cup salsa

Sauté the onion in the oil for 2 minutes until tender. Mix the garlic, tomatoes, chicken, sauce, chilies, ½ cup cheese, and cumin. Lay 2 tortillas in a round baking dish. Cover with half of the chicken mixture. Repeat. Cover with the last 2 tortillas, the salsa, and the remaining ½ cup cheese. Bake at 350 for 25 minutes.

SWEET AND SOUR CHICKEN

2 tablespoons brown sugar

4 teaspoons vinegar

1 8 oz can pineapple tidbits

Pineapple juice + water to make ¾ cup

Hot cooked rice

1 ½ tablespoons cornstarch

2 tablespoons prepared mustard

2 pouches chicken breast

1 2 oz jar diced pimentos, drained

Mix the sugar, cornstarch, vinegar, water, and mustard. Cook, stirring constantly, until it thickens. Cover and simmer for 10 more minutes. Stir in the chicken, pineapple, and pimentos. Cook until heated through. Serve over cooked rice.

NOTE: This is also good when served over chow mein noodles.

NOTE: One 13 oz can chicken breast may be used in the place of the pouches of chicken.

TERIYAKI CHICKEN WITH RICE

1 13 oz can chicken breast

1 tablespoon oil

1 4 oz can sliced mushrooms, drained

½ cup prepared teriyaki sauce

1 8 oz can pineapple tidbits, drained

½ cup chopped onion

1 2 oz jar chopped pimento, drained

1 can sliced water chestnuts, drained

¼ cup water

Hot cooked rice

Sauté the onion in the oil for 2 minutes until tender. Stir in the teriyaki sauce and the water. Add the chicken, mushrooms, chestnuts, pimento, and pineapple. Bring to a boil, reduce the heat, and simmer for 5 minutes. Serve over the rice.

THAI CHICKEN

2 pouches chicken breast

¼ cup creamy peanut butter

½ teaspoon garlic powder

¼ teaspoon ground ginger

½ cup chopped peanuts

1 can tomatoes with green chilies

2 tablespoons lime juice from bottle

1 tablespoon soy sauce

2 cups cooked rice

Mix the tomatoes, peanut butter, and the spices. Stir in the chicken. Bring to the boiling point and reduce the heat. Simmer, stirring frequently, for 10 minutes. Serve over the rice. Sprinkle with the peanuts before serving.

THAI CHICKEN AND PASTA

8 oz linguini or spaghetti

2 pouches chicken breast

½ teaspoon garlic powder

1 tablespoon cornstarch

1 chicken bouillon cube

1 14 oz can coconut milk (unsweetened)

½ teaspoon ground ginger

½ cup chopped peanuts

Cook the pasta in boiling water with the bouillon cube. Combine the coconut milk and the spices. Mix in the cornstarch. Stir in the chicken. Bring the mixture to a boil and reduce the heat. Simmer, uncovered, for 15 minutes. Drain the pasta and top with the chicken mixture. Sprinkle with the peanuts.

TROPICAL CHICKEN SALAD

1 13 oz can chicken breast

1/3 cup dry roasted peanuts

½ teaspoon curry powder

2 tablespoons reserved pineapple juice

1 8 oz can pineapple chunks, drained

1/4 cup mayonnaise

1 can Mandarin oranges, drained

Mix all ingredients. Serve with crackers, thinly sliced bread, or in tortilla cups (see Bread). This salad is also great when mounded on small plates and served as a lunch entrée.

COOKIES

Apricot and Coconut Balls

Brownies

Butter Nut Chewies

Butterscotch Haystacks

Cherry Cookie Bars

Chewy Peanut Macaroons

Chocolate Cake Cookies

Chocolate Chip Bar Cookies

Chocolate Peanut Butter Clusters

Easy Oatmeal Bars

Easy Peanut Butter Cookies

Magic Cookies

No Bake Cookies

Peanut Butter Bars

Peanut Butter Cookies

Peanut Cookies

Pistachio Cookies

APRICOT AND COCONUT BALLS

1 ½ cups of ground dried apricots   2 cups flaked coconut
2/3 cup milk powder   Powdered sugar

Combine the ground apricots, coconut, and milk powder. Shape into 1" balls. Roll in the powdered sugar and refrigerate.

BROWNIES

½ cup butter, softened   1 ½ cups sugar
½ cup cocoa powder   4 eggs
½ cup milk made from dry   1 1/3 cups self rising flour
2 teaspoons vanilla   ½ cup nuts, optional

Mix all ingredients and beat for 3 minutes. Pour into a 13 X 9 pan that has been coated with cooking spray. Bake at 350 for 20 to 25 minutes.

BUTTER NUT CHEWIES

½ cup butter   2 eggs
2 cups brown sugar   1 ½ cups self rising flour
1 teaspoon vanilla   1 cup chopped walnuts or pecans

Beat the eggs, butter, and sugar together. Blend in the flour. Add the vanilla and the nuts. Pour into a 13 X 9 pan that has been coated with cooking spray. Bake at 350 for 25 to 30 minutes.

BUTTERSCOTCH HAYSTACKS

1 11 oz package butterscotch chips   1 cup salted dry roasted peanuts
1 5 oz can chow mein noodles   1/3 cup creamy peanut butter

Melt the chips and the peanut butter together. Add the noodles and the peanuts, stirring until well mixed. Drop by teaspoons onto waxed paper. Let harden and store in an airtight container.

CHERRY COOKIE BARS

Crust:

1 2 layer box white cake mix	6 tablespoons butter, softened
1 cup oats	1 egg

Mix together and press into a 9 X 13" pan that has been coated with cooking spray.

Topping:

1 can cherry pie filling	½ cup chopped nuts
2 tablespoons butter, softened	¼ cup oats
½ cup brown sugar	

Pour the cherry pie filling over the crust. Mix the oats, butter, nuts, and brown sugar. Sprinkle over the pie filling. Bake at 350 for 35 to 40 minutes.

CHEWY PEANUT BUTTER MACAROONS

1 can sweetened condensed milk	½ cup creamy peanut butter
3 cups flaked coconut	

Mix all ingredients and drop by rounded teaspoons onto a baking sheet that has been lightly coated with cooking spray. Bake at 325 for 12 to 15 minutes.

CHOCOLATE CAKE COOKIES

1 box (2 layer size) chocolate cake mix	2 eggs, beaten
1 cup chocolate chips	½ cup quick cook oats
½ cup canola or vegetable oil	½ cup chopped nuts

Combine all ingredients and blend well. Drop by rounded teaspoons onto a baking sheet that has been coated with cooking spray. Bake at 350 for 8 to 10 minutes.

CHOCOLATE CHIP BAR COOKIES

Bottom layer:

½ cup butter, softened   ½ cup sugar
½ cup brown sugar   2 eggs, separated
1 tablespoon water   2 cups flour
1 teaspoon soda   ½ teaspoon salt

Beat the butter and the sugars together. Beat in the egg yolks, water, and dry ingredients. Pat the dough into the bottom of a 13 X 9 pan that has been coated with cooking spray.

Topping:

2 egg whites   ½ cup brown sugar
1 cup chocolate chips

Beat the egg whites until stiff. Slowly beat in the sugar. Stir in the chocolate chips. Put the mixture on top of the crust. Bake at 350 for 25 minutes.

CHOCOLATE PEANUT BUTTER CLUSTERS

1 cup semi sweet chocolate chips   2 cups peanut butter chips
1 cup salted dry roasted peanuts   1 cup ridged potato chips
½ cup pretzel sticks, broken into small pieces

Melt the chocolate and peanut butter chips together. Coarsely crush the potato chips. Stir in the remaining ingredients and drop by teaspoonfuls onto waxed paper. Let cool and store in an air tight container.

EASY OATMEAL BARS

2 cups oatmeal   1 cup self rising flour
1 cup sugar   1 tablespoon pancake syrup
¾ cup butter, softened

Mix all ingredients. The mixture will be very thick. Pour into a 13 X 9 pan that has been coated with cooking spray. Bake at 350 for 15 minutes. Cut into bars as soon as it comes out of the oven. Let cool before eating.

EASY PEANUT BUTTER COOKIES

1 cup crunchy peanut butter   1 cup sugar
1 egg, beaten

Mix the ingredients well. Drop by teaspoonfuls onto a baking sheet that has not been greased. Bake at 325 for 7 to 10 minutes. Let stand for 5 minutes before removing from the baking sheet.

MAGIC COOKIES

½ cup butter   1 ½ cups graham cracker crumbs
1 can sweetened condensed milk   1 cup chocolate chips
1 cup peanut butter chips   1 ½ cups flaked coconut
1 cup chopped pecans or walnuts

Melt the butter and mix with the graham cracker crumbs. Press into the bottom of a 13 X 9 baking dish. Pour the condensed milk over the crumb mixture. Sprinkle with the chips, then the coconut, then the nuts. Bake at 350 for 25 minutes. Let cool and cut into small bars.

NOTE: These cookies are very rich. They make nice gifts.

NO BAKE COOKIES

½ cup milk made from dry   2 cups sugar
3 tablespoons cocoa power   ½ cup butter
3 tablespoons creamy peanut butter   3 cups quick cook oats
1 teaspoon vanilla

Boil the milk, sugar, and cocoa for 2 minutes. Mix in the remaining ingredients and pour into an 8" square pan. Let cool and cut into squares.

PEANUT BUTTER BARS

½ cup creamy peanut butter

1 ½ cups sugar

1 teaspoon vanilla

½ cup butter

2 eggs

1 cup self rising flour

Microwave the peanut butter and the butter for 30 seconds. Stir and heat another 30 seconds. Stir in the sugar, eggs, vanilla, and flour. Pour into a 13 X 9" baking dish that has been coated with cooking spray. Bake at 350 for 25 to 30 minutes.

PEANUT BUTTER COOKIES

1 can sweetened condensed milk

2 cups baking mix

Sugar to coat

¾ cup creamy peanut butter

1 teaspoon vanilla

Beat the sweetened condensed milk and the peanut butter until mixture is smooth. Blend in the baking mix and the vanilla. Shape the cookies into 1" balls and roll in sugar. Put on a baking sheet that has not been greased. Flatten the cookies with the bottom of a glass and crisscross with the tines of a fork. Bake at 350 for 8 to 10 minutes until lightly browned.

PEANUT COOKIES

½ cup butter, softened

1 egg

1 cup all purpose flour

1 cup oats (quick cooking)

Coarse sugar crystals

¾ cup brown sugar

1 teaspoon vanilla

1 teaspoon baking powder

½ cup salted peanuts, chopped

Cream the butter and brown sugar. Beat in the egg and the vanilla. Stir in the remaining ingredients. Roll the dough into 1" balls. Roll the balls in the sugar crystals and put on a baking sheet. Slightly flatten the balls and bake at 350 for 10 to 12 minutes.

PISTACHIO COOKIES

2 eggs, beaten   1 package instant pistachio pudding mix
¾ baking mix   ¼ cup oil
½ teaspoon vanilla   ¼ cup finely chopped pecans or pistachios

Stir the dry ingredients together, then add the oil, eggs, and vanilla. Stir in the chopped nuts. Mix well. Using a small spoon, scoop out approximately 30 portions of dough. Put the dough on baking sheets which have not been greased. Flatten each scoop of dough to 2" size. Bake at 350 for 8 to 10 minutes.

NOTE: Try chocolate or chocolate fudge pudding mixes.

DESSERTS

Apple Cake

Applesauce Cake

Butterscotch Cake

Cherry Crunch Dessert

Chocolate Cherry Cake

Chocolate Cobbler

Chocolate Eggless Cake

Chocolate Syrup

Pineapple Cake

Preacher's Cake

Pumpkin Dump Cake

Pumpkin Pudding

Pumpkin Streusel

Seven-Up Cake

APPLE CAKE

1 box (2 layer size) spice cake mix

2 eggs

1 teaspoon vanilla

1 21 oz can apple pie filling

2 tablespoons canola or vegetable oil

½ cup chopped walnuts or pecans

Combine the cake mix, pie filling, eggs, oil, and vanilla. Beat on medium speed for 2 minutes. Stir in the nuts. Pour into a 13 X 9 pan that has been coated with cooking spray. Bake at 350 for 30 to 35 minutes.

APPLESAUCE CAKE

½ cup shortening

1 egg

2 cups all purpose flour

1 teaspoon baking soda

1 teaspoon ground cinnamon

½ cup finely chopped nuts

1 cup sugar

1 cup canned applesauce

1 teaspoon salt

1 teaspoon baking powder

¼ teaspoon nutmeg

Cream the shortening and the sugar. Add the egg and beat. Stir in the applesauce. Mix the dry ingredients and stir into the batter. Stir in the nuts. Pour into an 8" baking dish that has been coated with cooking spray. Bake at 350 for 50 minutes until a toothpick inserted into the middle comes out clean.

BUTTERSCOTCH CAKE

1 box cook and serve butterscotch pudding mix

1 box (2 layer size) yellow cake mix

½ cup chopped walnuts or pecans

2 cups milk made from dry

1 cup butterscotch chips

Combine the pudding mix and the milk. Cook as directed. Stir in the dry cake mix, chips, and nuts. Bake in a 13 X 9 pan that has been coated with cooking spray. Bake at 350 for 35 to 40 minutes.

CHERRY CRUNCH DESSERT

1 box (single layer size) yellow cake mix

¼ cup melted butter

½ cup chopped walnuts or pecans

1 can cherry pie filling

Combine the cake mix, nuts, and melted butter. Pour the pie filling into an 8" baking dish that has been coated with cooking spray. Sprinkle the cake mix mixture over and bake at 350 for 20 to 25 minutes and lightly browned.

CHOCOLATE CHERRY CAKE

1 box (2 layer size) chocolate cake mix
1 teaspoon almond flavoring
1 can cherry pie filling

2 eggs, beaten
1 teaspoon vanilla

Stir all ingredients until blended. Pour into a 13 X 9 baking dish that has been coated with cooking spray. Bake at 350 for 25 minutes.

CHOCOLATE COBBLER

1 cup self rising flour
¼ cup + 2 tablespoons cocoa
1 cup brown sugar
2 tablespoons oil
1 ¾ cup hot water

½ cup sugar
2 tablespoons oil
½ cup milk made from dry
1 cup brown sugar

Combine the flour, sugar, and 2 tablespoons of the cocoa. Stir in the milk and oil until the mixture is smooth. Pour into an 8" baking dish that has been coated with cooking spray. Combine the ¼ cup cocoa and the brown sugar and sprinkle over the batter. Pour the hot water over the batter. DO NOT STIR. Bake at 350 for 40 to 45 minutes until the top of the cake springs back when lightly touched.

CHOCOLATE EGGLESS CAKE

3 cups all purpose flour
1/3 cup unsweetened cocoa powder
1 teaspoon salt
¾ cup canola or vegetable oil
2 teaspoons vinegar

2 cups sugar
2 teaspoons baking soda
2 cups water
2 teaspoons vanilla

Combine the flour, sugar, cocoa, baking soda, and salt. Add the oil and water. Mix well (the batter is thin). Stir in the vanilla and the vinegar. Pour into a 13 X 9" pan that has been coated with cooking spray. Bake at 350 for 25 to 30 minutes. Cool completely before cutting.

NOTE: If desired, top each serving of the cake with chocolate syrup (See recipe that follows).

CHOCOLATE SYRUP

1 cup unsweetened cocoa powder

1 cup water

2 teaspoons vanilla

1 ½ cups sugar

½ teaspoon salt

Combine all ingredients and bring to a near boil. Reduce the heat and simmer for at least 1 minute. Simmering for additional time will result in a thicker syrup.

NOTE: This syrup is good served over chocolate, white, or yellow cakes. It is also good served over pancakes.

PINEAPPLE CAKE

1 box (1 layer size) yellow cake mix

1 box instant vanilla pudding mix

½ teaspoon pineapple flavoring

1 8 oz can undrained crushed pineapple

1 ½ cups milk made from dry

Prepare the cake mix as directed and bake in an 8" baking dish that has been coated with cooking spray. With a toothpick or wooden skewer, poke holes in the cake and pour the pineapple and juice over the cake. Cool. Combine the pudding mix, milk, and flavoring. Beat until thickened and pour over the cake. Refrigerate before serving.

PREACHER'S CAKE

This is named Preacher's cake since the ingredients are 2 by 2 by 2, just like the animals on Noah's ark.

2 cups sugar

2 teaspoons vanilla

½ cup chopped walnuts or pecans

1 can cream cheese frosting

2 cups self rising flour

2 eggs

1 20 oz can crushed pineapple, not drained

Mix all the ingredients except the frosting and pour into a 13 X 9 pan that has been coated with cooking spray. Bake at 350 for 45 minutes. Let the cake cool and frost with the cream cheese frosting.

PUMPKIN DUMP CAKE

1 29 oz can pumpkin puree (not pie filling)

1 12 oz can evaporated milk

1 teaspoon salt

1 2 layer size box yellow cake mix

¾ cup butter

1 cup sugar

2 teaspoons cinnamon

3 eggs

1 cup chopped nuts

Mix the pumpkin, milk, sugar, cinnamon, and eggs. Pour into a 13 X 9" pan that has been coated with cooking spray. Sprinkle the dry cake mix over the mixture. Sprinkle with the chopped nuts. Melt the butter and pour evenly over the nuts. Bake at 350 for 50 minutes.

PUMPKIN PUDDING

2 boxes instant vanilla pudding mix

1 cup canned pumpkin

2 cups milk made from dry

½ teaspoon cinnamon

Beat all ingredients together until mixture begins to thicken. Pour into small plastic glasses or containers. Chill.

PUMPKIN STREUSEL CAKE

1 box (2 layer size) yellow cake mix

3 beaten eggs

1 teaspoon vanilla

1 16 oz can pumpkin

¼ cup butter

Topping:

1 cup brown sugar

½ cup chopped walnuts

2 teaspoons cinnamon

¼ cup butter

Combine the cake mix, pumpkin, eggs, and vanilla and beat well. Pour half of the mixture into a 13 X 9 cake pan that has been coated with cooking spray. Combine the topping ingredients and sprinkle half over the cake batter. Repeat. Bake at 350 for 40 to 45 minutes.

SEVEN-UP CAKE

1 2-layer size package yellow cake mix
¾ cup canola or vegetable oil
1 12 oz can 7 Up
½ cup chopped nuts

1 package vanilla instant pudding mix
3 eggs
½ cup flaked coconut

Mix all ingredients. Pour into a 13 X 9 pan that has been coated with cooking spray. Bake at 350 for 45 minutes.

Topping:
2 envelopes whipped topping mix
1 package Vanilla instant pudding mix

1 ½ cups milk made from dry

Beat all ingredients and spread onto the cake. Refrigerate.

HAM (CANNED AND COUNTRY HAM)

Almost Breakfast Sausage

Baked Ham

BBQ Ham

Cheesy Ham and Rice

Country Ham and Asparagus

Country Ham and Red Eye Gravy

Country Ham and Rice

Country Ham in Mustard Sauce

Country Ham Spaghetti

Country Ham with Cheesy Spaghetti

Creamed Ham

Ham and Pasta Salad

Ham Casserole

Ham Enchiladas

Ham Haystack

Ham and Vegetable Bake

Ham Balls

"Ham" Burgers

Ham Burritos

Ham Loaf

Ham Pot Pie

Ham with Mandarin Oranges

Ham with Cherry Sauce

Ham with Mustard Gravy

Ham with Peach Sauce

Ham with Sauerkraut and Vegetables

Impossible Country Ham Pizza

Penne and Country Ham

Pineapple and Ham Kebobs

Sweet and Sour Ham

Tangy Ham Steaks

ALMOST BREAKFAST SAUSAGE

1 6 oz can ham
1 egg, beaten
1 tablespoon oil for frying

3 tablespoons chicken flavored stuffing mix
1/8 teaspoon rubbed sage

Crush the stuffing mix. Combine the ham, stuffing mix, egg, and sage. Mix well and shape into 3 patties. Fry in the oil for 2 to 3 minutes per side until browned.

BAKED HAM

1 16 oz canned ham
¼ cup brown sugar

1 to 2 tablespoons spicy mustard

Coat the canned ham with the mustard. Press the brown sugar into the mustard. Bake uncovered at 350 for 20 o 25 minutes.

BBQ HAM

1 16 oz canned ham
½ teaspoon dry mustard
½ teaspoon onion powder

¾ cup prepared BBQ sauce
½ teaspoon garlic powder
½ teaspoon smoke flavoring

Slice the ham and cut into bite sized pieces. Combine the BBQ sauce and the spices and bring to a boil. Reduce the heat and stir in the ham. Simmer, uncovered, for 10 minutes. Serve on slices of bread as open faced sandwiches or on buns as sandwiches.

CHEESY HAM AND RICE

1 cup canned ham, diced
1 cup processed cheese food, grated
1 4 oz can sliced mushrooms, drained
Hot cooked rice

1 can cream of chicken soup
1 teaspoon dried chives
½ cup canned mixed vegetables, drained

Combine the ham, soup, cheese, chives, mushrooms, and vegetables. Heat to boiling and reduce the heat. Simmer for 5 minutes and serve over the rice.

NOTE: This is also good served over chow mein noodles.

COUNTRY HAM AND ASPARAGUS

1 cup country ham or canned ham, diced

1 4 oz can sliced mushrooms, drained

2 cups corkscrew pasta, cooked

¾ cup round buttery cracker crumbs

1 can asparagus

1 can cream of chicken soup

¼ cup butter

Drain the asparagus and cut into 1" pieces. Mix the asparagus, diced ham, mushrooms, cooked pasta, and soup. Pour into a baking dish that has been coated with cooking spray. Melt the butter and stir into the cracker crumbs. Sprinkle the crumb mixture over the casserole. Bake at 350 for 30 minutes.

COUNTRY HAM AND RED EYE GRAVY

2 slices country ham

1 cup brewed coffee

Put the ham slices into a hot skillet that has been coated with cooking spray. Cook on medium heat for 1 ½ minutes on each side. Remove from the skillet and stir in the coffee. Pour the red eye gravy over the ham slices when served.

COUNTRY HAM AND RICE

1 cup country ham slices, diced

1 can cream of chicken soup

1 can peas and carrots, drained

1 4 oz can sliced mushrooms, drained

½ cup water

1 package yellow rice mix

Prepare the rice mix as directed on the package. Dice the ham. Mix the ham, soup, water, and vegetables. Bring to a boil. Reduce the heat and simmer for 5 minutes. Serve over the rice.

COUNTRY HAM IN MUSTARD SAUCE

1 cup country ham slices, diced

1 teaspoon lemon juice

½ cup water

Hot cooked rice or pasta

2 tablespoons spicy mustard

1 can cream of chicken soup

1 can artichoke hearts

Drain the artichoke hearts and chop. Mix the soup, water, and mustard and heat to a boil. Reduce the heat and stir in the country ham and artichokes. Reduce the heat and simmer for 5 minutes. Serve over the rice or pasta.

COUNTRY HAM SPAGHETTI

3 cups cooked spaghetti

1 cup grated Cheddar cheese

1 14 oz jar spaghetti sauce

½ teaspoon onion powder

1 tablespoon grated Parmesan cheese

1 chicken bouillon cube

1 cup country ham, cut into bite sized pieces

½ teaspoon garlic powder

½ teaspoon pepper

Cook the pasta in boiling water with the bouillon cube. Mix the spaghetti sauce with the spices. Mix in the country ham, cheese, and pasta. Sprinkle with the Parmesan cheese. Bake at 350 for 25 to 30 minutes until bubbly.

COUNTRY HAM WITH CHEESY SPAGHETTI

8 oz uncooked spaghetti

1 tablespoon canola or olive oil

1 teaspoon dried chives

5 slices processed cheese food

1 cup country ham cut into bite sized pieces

1 chicken bouillon cube

1 teaspoon garlic powder

1 can cream of chicken soup

½ cup water

1 can sliced mushrooms, drained

Cook the spaghetti in boiling water with the bouillon cube. Mix the oil, garlic, and chives together and toss with the hot, drained spaghetti. Mix the soup, cheese slices, and water and cook on medium heat for 5 minutes until the cheese has melted. Stir in the ham and mushrooms and cook 5 minutes. Stir in the spaghetti and cook until heated through.

CREAMED HAM

1 cup thinly sliced, then diced canned ham

1 4 oz can sliced mushrooms, drained

1/2 cup milk made from dry

1 cup canned peas, drained

1 can cream of chicken soup

Salt, pepper to taste

Mix the soup and the milk. Stir in the ham, peas, and mushrooms. Heat over medium heat for 10 minutes. Stir in the salt and pepper. Serve over rice, noodles, toast, or mashed potatoes.

HAM AND PASTA SALAD

2 cups cooked spiral pasta

¼ cup chopped onion

1/3 cup prepared Italian salad dressing

2 teaspoons spicy mustard

1 cup canned ham

1 4 oz can black olives, drained

2 tablespoons mayonnaise

Salt, pepper to taste

Slice the ham into thin slices and then into bite-sized pieces. Mix the onion, olives, Italian dressing, mayonnaise, salt, and pepper. Combine the ham and the pasta, pour the sauce over and mix well. Chill before serving.

HAM CASSEROLE

1 can green beans, drained

1 cup canned ham

Grated Cheddar cheese

1 can cream of chicken soup

Chow mein noodles

Slice the ham into thin slices and then into bite-sized pieces. Mix the ham, green beans, and soup and cook over medium heat for 10 minutes until heated, stirring frequently. Serve over the chow mein noodles and top with the grated cheese.

NOTE: Rice or cooked noodles may be substituted for the chow mein noodles.

HAM ENCHILADAS

1 cup diced canned ham

1 4 ½ oz can chopped green chilies, drained

1 can cream of chicken soup

½ teaspoon onion powder

6 flour tortillas

½ cup salsa

¾ cup grated Cheddar cheese, divided

½ teaspoon garlic powder

½ teaspoon chili powder

Mix the ham, salsa, chilies, and ½ cup of the cheese. Divide evenly among the tortillas. Roll the tortillas and put into a baking dish that has been coated with cooking spray. Mix the soup and spices and pour over the tortillas. Bake at 350 for 20 to 25 minutes until bubbly. Top with the ¼ cup cheese and bake for 5 more minutes.

HAM HAYSTACKS

2 cups cooked rice

1 can cream of chicken soup

1 cup crushed pineapple

Grated cheese

Salsa

1 can chow mein noodles

1 cup canned ham

¼ cup pineapple juice

Coconut

Mix the soup and the pineapple juice and heat. Slice the ham very thin and cut into bite-sized pieces. Stir into the soup and heat. On each plate, put a small amount of the chow mein noodles, then the rice, then the ham mixture. Top with the pineapple, then the cheese, then the coconut. Pour on a small amount of the salsa.

HAM AND VEGETABLE BAKE

1 cup canned ham, diced

½ cup grated Cheddar cheese

1½ cups milk made from dry

1 teaspoon paprika

½ teaspoon pepper

1 can mixed vegetables, drained

½ cup baking mix

2 teaspoons spicy mustard

½ teaspoon dried parsley flakes

2 eggs, beaten

Mix the diced ham and the vegetables. Beat the remaining ingredients together and combine with the ham. Pour into a baking dish that has been coated with cooking spray. Bake at 350 for 45 minutes.

HAM BALLS

Ham balls:

1 16 oz canned ham

1 egg, beaten

¼ teaspoon pepper

1 cup Chicken flavored stuffing mix

2 teaspoons spicy mustard

Sauce:

¾ cup brown sugar

3 tablespoons white vinegar

1/3 cup water

½ teaspoon dry mustard

Mash the ham with a fork. Mix the ham, stuffing mix, beaten egg, mustard, and pepper. Shape the ham mixture into 1" balls. Put into an 8" baking dish that has been coated with cooking spray.

Mix the sauce ingredients and bring to a boil. Reduce the heat and simmer uncovered for 4 minutes. Pour over the ham balls and bake at 350 for 25 to 30 minutes, basting several times with the sauce.

NOTE: An 8 oz can of drained pineapple chunks may be added to the baking dish before baking.

"HAM" BURGERS

1 8 oz can of ham   1 egg, beaten
¼ cup crushed saltine crackers   ½ teaspoon chicken bouillon granules
½ teaspoon pepper   ¼ cup finely chopped onion

Mash the ham with a fork. Mix the egg, crackers, and seasonings. Mix in the ham and shape into 3 to 4 patties. Fry in a lightly greased skillet until golden brown.

NOTE: Mustard or a cheese sauce is good with these burgers.

HAM BURRITOS

1 cup canned ham, diced   1 cup cooked rice
½ cup salsa   1 4 ½ oz can chopped green chilies, drained
1 cup grated Cheddar cheese   ¼ cup finely chopped onion
5 to 6 flour tortillas

Combine the diced ham, rice, salsa, chilies, cheese, and onion. Divide among the tortillas. Tuck the ends of the tortillas in and roll. Place seam side down in a skillet and cook for 10 minutes, turning them so that they are very lightly browned.

HAM LOAF

HAM LOAF:

1 16 oz canned ham

1 egg, beaten

¼ teaspoon pepper

1 ½ cup Chicken flavored stuffing mix

2 teaspoons spicy mustard

TOPPING:

½ cup applesauce

1 tablespoon brown sugar

1 tablespoon spicy mustard

1 tablespoon vinegar

Mash the ham with a fork. Stir in the stuffing mix, beaten egg, mustard, and pepper. Mix well. Coat a baking dish with cooking spray. Shape the ham loaf into an oval shape. With your fingers, make a ¾" rim around the top of the ham loaf to make an indention for the topping.

Mix all ingredients for the topping and spoon into the indention. Bake at 350 for 1 hour.

NOTE: This ham loaf may be made without the topping.
NOTE: It is good the next day sliced for sandwiches.

HAM POT PIE

1 cup self rising flour

1 cup milk made from dry

1 can cut green beans

1 can cream of chicken soup

½ cup melted butter

2 cups canned ham, cubed

1 can whole potatoes, drained

Mix the flour, melted butter, and milk. Dice the potatoes. Mix the potatoes, ham, green beans, and soup. Pour into a baking dish that has been coated with cooking spray. Pour the flour batter over the ham mixture. Bake at 350 for 35 to 45 minutes until the top crust is lightly browned.

HAM WITH MANDARIN ORANGES

1 16 oz canned ham

2 tablespoons brown sugar

2 tablespoons spicy mustard

1 can Mandarin oranges, drained

Slice the ham into 4 ham steaks. Brown the ham steaks in a lightly greased skillet. Turn the ham steaks over and remove from the heat. Spread the mustard on the ham steaks, sprinkle with the brown sugar, and cover with the orange segments. Cover the skillet with aluminum foil and cook on low heat for 10 minutes. Remove the foil and cook for 2 more minutes.

HAM WITH CHERRY SAUCE

1 16 oz canned ham   ½ cup cherry preserves
¼ cup hot pepper jelly

Cut the ham into 4 steaks. Sauté in a lightly greased skillet until lightly browned on both sides. Mix the cherry preserves and the hot pepper jelly and heat on low heat until bubbly, stirring frequently. Serve the sauce over the ham steaks.

HAM WITH MUSTARD GRAVY

1 16 oz canned ham   ½ teaspoon chicken bouillon granules
½ teaspoon pepper   2 tablespoons butter
1 tablespoon prepared spicy mustard   1 cup chicken broth
1 teaspoon dried parsley flakes   2 tablespoons flour

Cut the ham into 4 ham steaks. Fry the ham steaks until lightly browned on both sides. Remove the ham from the skillet and melt the butter. Stir in the flour and whisk until smooth; slowly add the broth and spices. Whisk until smooth and cook on medium heat for 4 to 5 minutes until the mixture begins to thicken. Serve the mustard sauce over the ham steaks.

HAM WITH PEACH SAUCE

1 16 oz canned ham   ¼ cup sugar
¼ cup salsa   2 teaspoons lemon juice
1 teaspoon Worcestershire sauce   ½ teaspoon chili powder
½ teaspoon garlic powder   ¼ cup water
1 can peach slices, drained and diced

Cut the ham into 4 ham steaks. Sauté in a lightly greased skillet until lightly browned on both sides. Mix the sugar, salsa, lemon juice, water and spices and bring to a boil. Reduce the heat and simmer for 15 minutes, stirring frequently. Add the peaches and cook until heated through. Serve the sauce over the ham steaks.

HAM WITH SAUERKRAUT AND VEGETABLES

1 can sauerkraut, well drained

1 can whole potatoes

¼ teaspoon pepper

1 can whole or crinkle cut carrots

1 16 oz canned ham

Coat a slow cooker with cooking spray. Imagine it being divided into thirds. Mound the sauerkraut into one third, the potatoes into one third, and the carrots into one third. Sprinkle with the pepper. Cover with the ham. Cook on low for 4 to 6 hours or on high for 2 to 3 hours.

NOTE: This may also be layered and baked, covered, at 350 for 30 to 40 minutes.

IMPOSSIBLE COUNTRY HAM PIZZA

First layer:

½ cup chopped onion

1/3 cup grated Parmesan cheese

Second layer:

1½ cups milk made from dry

¾ cup baking mix

3 eggs

Topping:

1 cup tomato sauce

½ teaspoon Italian seasoning

¼ cup chopped onion

½ teaspoon garlic powder

½ cup chopped country ham

1 cup grated Cheddar cheese

Liberally coat a 10" pie plate with cooking spray. Sprinkle the first layer of onions and cheese.

Beat the milk, eggs, and baking mix for 1 minute with a whisk until smooth. Pour over the onions and bake at 350 for 20 minutes. Mix the tomato sauce and the spices and pour over the crust. Top with the country ham and the onions. Sprinkle with the cheese and bake at 350 for 15 minutes. Allow to cool for 5 minutes before cutting

PENNE AND COUNTRY HAM

2 cups penne pasta, cooked

1 can cream of celery soup

½ cup bite size pieces country ham

½ cup milk made from dry

½ cup canned peas, drained

½ teaspoon pepper

1 can sliced mushrooms, drained

½ cup grated Cheddar cheese

Cook the pasta and drain. Mix the pasta, soup, milk, peas, mushrooms, and pepper and cook on medium heat for 15 minutes, stirring frequently. Sprinkle the cheese over each serving.

PINEAPPLE AND HAM KEBOBS

1 16 oz canned ham

¾ cup prepared BBQ sauce

1 20 oz can pineapple chunks

skewers

Cut the canned ham into 1" cubes. Drain the pineapple chunks. Put all ingredients into a plastic bag and refrigerate for at least 4 hours. Thread the ham and the pineapple onto the skewers and grill or broil until heated through.

SWEET AND SOUR HAM

2 tablespoons brown sugar

4 teaspoons vinegar

Pineapple juice + water to make ¾ cup

1 9 oz can pineapple tidbits, drained

1 ½ tablespoons cornstarch

2 tablespoons prepared mustard

2 cups canned ham, cut into ½" cubes

1 2 oz jar diced pimentos, drained

Mix the sugar, cornstarch, vinegar, water, and mustard. Cook, stirring constantly, until it thickens. Cover and simmer for 10 more minutes. Stir in the ham, pineapple, and pimentos. Cook until heated through. Serve over cooked rice.

NOTE: This is also good when served over chow mein noodles.

TANGY HAM STEAKS

1 16 oz canned ham

½ cup canned cranberry sauce

1 tablespoon vinegar

2 teaspoons oil

1 tablespoon prepared mustard

Cut the ham into 4 ham steaks and brown in the oil. Remove the ham steaks and mix the cranberry sauce, mustard, and vinegar. Bring to the boiling point, turn down the heat and simmer for 5 minutes. Serve over the ham steaks.

MEATLESS ENTREES

Asparagus Quiche

BBQ Beans over Rice

Black Bean and Pasta Salad

Black Bean Tostadas

Cheesy Pasta and Vegetables

Golden Stew

Lemon Spaghetti

Lentil or Pinto Bean Burgers

Macaroni and Cheese

Mexican Lasagna

Mexican Pizza

Penne Pasta with Vodka

Pimento Cheese

Pineapple and Black Bean Enchiladas

Red Beans and Yellow Rice

Vegetable Quiche

Vegetables with Pasta

Walnut Linguini

Welsh Rarebit Sauce

Yellow Rice Taco Salad

ASPARAGUS QUICHE

1 saltine cracker pie crust (See Pies)
½ cup chopped onion
3 eggs, beaten
½ cup grated Parmesan cheese

1 can asparagus, drained
2 tablespoons butter
¾ cup evaporated milk
1 cup grated Cheddar cheese

Press the cracker crust into the bottom of a pie plate. Bake the crust at 350 for 8 minutes. Cut the asparagus into 1" pieces. Sauté the onion in the butter for 2 minutes until tender. Beat the eggs and milk together. Stir all ingredients and pour into the crust. Bake at 375 for 45 minutes until set. Let this cool for 20 minutes before slicing.

BBQ BEANS OVER RICE

2 cans pinto or black beans, rinsed and drained
½ teaspoon garlic powder
1 teaspoon dried parsley flakes

½ cup prepared BBQ sauce
½ teaspoon onion powder
3 cups cooked rice

Mix the BBQ sauce and the spices. Stir in the drained beans and heat until boiling. Serve the bean mixture over the cooked rice.

BLACK BEAN AND PASTA SALAD

1 ½ cups uncooked corkscrew pasta
½ cup ranch salad dressing made from dry mix
½ teaspoon garlic powder
½ teaspoon dried cilantro
1 8 oz can pineapple chunks
½ cup grated Cheddar cheese

2 tablespoons lime juice
1 teaspoon chili powder
½ teaspoon onion powder
1 can black beans, drained
1 4 oz can black olives, drained

Cook the pasta as directed on the package. Drain well and cool. Make the ranch dressing as directed on the package. Mix ½ cup of the dressing, the lime juice, and the spices. Combine the cooled pasta, the black beans, pineapple chunks, olives, and cheese. Stir the sauce into the pasta mixture. Chill at least 1 hour before serving.

BLACK BEAN TOSTADAS

4 corn tortillas

1 can black beans, rinsed and drained

½ teaspoon garlic powder

1 teaspoon lime juice from bottle

¼ cup prepared salsa or taco sauce

¼ cup oil

½ teaspoon cumin

½ teaspoon chili powder

½ cup grated Cheddar cheese

Put the oil into a skillet and fry the corn tortillas one at a time for 2 minutes on each side until crispy. Drain on paper towels. Combine the beans, spices, and lime juice and divide the mixture over the tostadas. Sprinkle with the cheese. Top each tostada with 1 tablespoon of the salsa.

CHEESY PASTA AND VEGETABLES

2 ½ cups cooked pasta

¼ cup milk made from dry

1 teaspoon chicken bouillon granules

1 can mixed vegetables, drained

8 oz processed cheese food

1 tablespoon ketchup

1 prepared mustard

1 can sliced mushrooms, drained

Combine the milk and cheese with the bouillon, ketchup, and mustard. Cook on medium heat until the cheese has melted and the mixture is bubbly. Stir in the pasta, mushrooms, and mixed vegetables and mix well. Cook 5 more minutes, stirring frequently.

GOLDEN STEW

1 can canned crinkle cut carrots, drained

1 can peas, drained

2 tablespoons oil

8 oz processed cheese food, cubed

1 can whole potatoes, drained

½ cup chopped onion

1 can cream of celery soup

2 cups water

Cut the potatoes into cubes. Sauté the onion in the oil for 2 minutes until tender. Mix all ingredients and cook on medium heat until thoroughly heated.

LEMON SPAGHETTI

1 16 oz package spaghetti or linguini
1 ½ cups prepared Alfredo sauce
2 teaspoons dried parsley flakes
¼ cup grated Parmesan cheese

2 chicken bouillon cubes
1 teaspoon garlic powder
3 to 4 tablespoons lemon juice
salt, pepper to taste

Cook the pasta in boiling water with the bouillon cubes. Drain. Mix the Alfredo sauce with the remaining ingredients and toss with the pasta.

LENTIL OR PINTO BEAN BURGERS

2 cans lentils or pinto beans, rinsed and drained
1 cup saltine cracker crumbs
Salt, pepper to taste
Flour to coat

1 cup finely chopped onion
1 beaten egg
2 drops hot sauce if desired

Mash the beans slightly. Mix the beans, onion, cracker crumbs, egg, and spices. Shape into patties. Gently coat the patties with flour. Fry in a lightly greased skillet for 5 minutes per side until lightly browned.

MACARONI AND CHEESE

1 16 oz box of macaroni
2 cups grated Cheddar cheese
2 eggs
Salt, pepper to taste

1 chicken bouillon cube
1 cup milk made from dry
2 tablespoons butter

Put the bouillon cube in boiling water. Add the macaroni and cook as directed. Drain the macaroni. Add the butter and mix until melted. Beat the eggs into the milk. Add the salt, and pepper. Pour this over the macaroni. Spoon into a baking dish. Top with the grated cheese. Bake at 350 for 25 to 30 minutes.

MEXICAN LASAGNA

1 can black beans, rinsed and drained
1 can diced tomatoes
½ teaspoon dried basil, crushed
½ teaspoon cilantro
1 cup grated Cheddar cheese

1 cup canned corn, drained
1 teaspoon garlic powder
1 teaspoon cumin
1 teaspoon onion powder
4 6" corn tortillas

Mix the beans, corn, tomatoes, and spices. Put 2 tortillas in a round greased baking dish. Cover with half of the bean mixture and half of the cheese. Repeat the layers. Bake at 350 for 30 minutes. Let this set for 5 minutes before serving.

MEXICAN PIZZA

1 package Mexican corn bread mix
¾ cup grated Cheddar cheese, divided
1 can black beans, rinsed and drained

½ cup taco sauce
1 8 oz can pineapple tidbits, drained

Make the Mexican corn bread mix as directed. Coat a 12" pizza pan with cooking spray. Spread the corn bread evenly on the pan and bake at 350 for 8 to 10 minutes. Spoon on the taco sauce and ½ cup of the cheese. Top with the black beans and the pineapple. Sprinkle with the remaining ¼ cup of the cheese. Bake at 350 for 8 to 10 minutes until the cheese is bubbly.

PENNE PASTA WITH VODKA

1 16 oz package penne pasta
½ cup chopped onion
1 teaspoon garlic powder
1 teaspoon dried parsley flakes
½ cup water
1 can cream of mushroom soup

2 chicken bouillon cubes
2 tablespoons butter
½ teaspoon dried red pepper flakes
1/2 cup vodka or chicken broth
1 14 oz can crushed tomatoes
Grated Parmesan cheese

Cook the pasta in boiling water with the bouillon cubes. Drain. Sauté the onion in the butter for 2 minutes until tender. Mix the onion, spices, tomatoes, and soup. Stir in the vodka. Simmer for 10 minutes, until heated through. Serve the pasta topped with the sauce and topped with the cheese.

PIMENTO CHEESE

½ cup grated Cheddar cheese
¼ cup mayonnaise
1 tablespoon prepared ranch dressing

½ cup grated processed cheese food
1 2 oz jar chopped pimentos, drained

Mix the mayonnaise and ranch dressing and mix with the other ingredients. This makes a great sandwich spread for cold or grilled pimento cheese sandwiches.

PINEAPPLE AND BLACK BEAN ENCHILADAS

½ cup chopped onion
1 8 oz can crushed pineapple
1 4 ½ oz can green chilies
½ teaspoon garlic powder
½ teaspoon pepper
4 flour tortillas

1 tablespoon oil
¾ cup canned black beans, drained
½ teaspoon dried cilantro
½ teaspoon cumin
¾ cup salsa, divided
½ cup grated Cheddar cheese

Sauté the onion in the oil for 2 minutes until tender. Drain the pineapple and reserve 2 tablespoons of the juice. Mix the onion, pineapple, beans, chilies, spices, and ¼ cup of the salsa. Divide among the tortillas. Roll the tortillas up and put into a baking dish that has been coated with cooking spray. Mix the reserved pineapple juice, ½ cup of the salsa and pour over the enchiladas. Bake at 350 for 25 minutes. Top with the cheese and bake 5 more minutes.

RED BEANS AND YELLOW RICE

1 10 oz package yellow rice mix
1 tablespoon oil
1 can diced tomatoes
½ teaspoon cumin
Salt, pepper to taste

½ cup chopped onion
2 cans red beans, rinsed and drained
1 teaspoon garlic powder
1 teaspoon dried parsley flakes

Cook the rice as directed on the package. Sauté the onion in the oil for 2 minutes until tender. Combine the beans, tomatoes, and spices and cook, uncovered, over medium heat for 10 minutes, stirring frequently. For each serving, put rice on a plate and top with the bean mixture.

VEGETABLE QUICHE

1 unbaked pie crust
1 can sliced mushrooms, drained
2 tablespoons butter
1 cup grated Cheddar cheese
½ teaspoon garlic powder
½ teaspoon dried parsley flakes

1 can mixed vegetables, drained
½ cup chopped onion
6 eggs
½ teaspoon chicken bouillon granules
1 teaspoon dried chives

Put the pie crust into the pie plate and prick with a fork. Bake at 350 for 12 minutes. Beat the eggs well. Stir in the remaining ingredients and pour into the pie crust. Bake at 350 for 45 minutes until set. Let stand 20 minutes before slicing.

VEGETABLES WITH PASTA

1 can mixed vegetables, drained
1 can cream of celery soup
½ teaspoon garlic powder
Hot cooked pasta

1 4 oz can sliced mushrooms, drained
½ cup water
½ teaspoon pepper
Grated Parmesan cheese

Combine the vegetables, soup, water, and spices. Bring to a boil. Reduce the heat to medium and cook for 5 minutes. Serve over the pasta. Top each serving with Parmesan cheese.

WALNUT LINGUINI

2 teaspoons dried minced garlic
1 tablespoon dried parsley flakes
3 tablespoons olive or canola oil
12 oz linguini
Salt, pepper to taste

¾ cup chopped English walnuts
2/3 cup grated Parmesan cheese
1 teaspoon dried basil
1 chicken bouillon cube

Cook the linguini in boiling water with the bouillon cube. Drain well. Sauté the garlic and the walnuts in the oil until the walnuts are lightly toasted. Add all ingredients to the skillet and toss to coat.

WELSH RAREBIT SAUCE

2 tablespoons butter
3 tablespoons all purpose flour
1 12 oz can beer or milk made from dry
2 drops hot sauce

2 tablespoons vegetable or canola oil
1 tablespoon dry mustard
2 cups grated Cheddar cheese
Salt, pepper to taste

Melt the butter and oil. Mix the flour and the dry mustard into the butter mixture. Cook for 1 minute. Add the liquid and whisk until smooth. Cook over medium heat 5 minutes until thickened. Stir in the cheese and seasonings and cook over very low heat for 5 to 10 minutes until the cheese is thickened.

NOTE: This sauce is equally good when served over salmon loaf, salmon or tuna cakes, or when stirred into cooked macaroni.

YELLOW RICE TACO SALAD

1 5 oz package yellow rice
1 can Mandarin orange slices, drained
½ cup taco sauce

1 8 oz can pineapple tidbits
1 cup canned black beans, drained

Drain the pineapple tidbits and reserve the juice. Use the juice instead of part of the water called for in the yellow rice. Cook the rice as directed on the package. Cool slightly. Stir in the taco sauce. Mix well, then stir in the remaining ingredients. Serve hot or at room temperature.

OTHER MEATS

BACON

Bacon and Cheese Rarebit

Bacon and Pineapple Pizza

Bacon Pie

Bacon Quiche

Cheese & Bacon Sandwich

Pasta with Bacon and Vegetables

Pork Roast and Vegetables

CHILI

Chili Mac in Bowl

Chili Pot Pie

Chili Shepherd's Pie

Chili Topped Spaghetti

Chuck Wagon Stew

Summer Sausage Fried Rice

CORNED BEEF

Corned Beef Dinner

Corned Beef Hash

Corned Beef Salad

Corned Beef Sandwich

Reuben Casserole

PEPPERONI

Peppy Macaroni Casserole

Pepperoni and Pasta Salad

Pepperoni Pie

Pepperoni Pizza

Pepperoni Quesadillas

Pizza Casserole

PORK ROAST

Open Faced Roast Pork Sandwiches

Pork and Beans

Pork and Stuffing

Pork and Sweet Potatoes

Pork BBQ

Pork Roast and Dried Fruit

Pork Stew

Pork with Sauerkraut

Spicy Pork

SUMMER SAUSAGE

Sausage Beer Soup

Summer Sausage Quesadillas

Summer Sausage Reuben

Summer Sausage/Mushrooms

BACON

BACON AND CHEESE RAREBIT

Rarebit sauce (See Meatless Entrees)   3 slices precooked bacon per sandwich
1 slice toasted bread per sandwich   1 tablespoon salsa per sandwich

Toast the bread slices. Top each slice with 3 slices of precooked bacon and ¼ cup of the rarebit sauce.
Drain the liquid from the salsa and sprinkle over the sandwich. Serve hot.

BACON AND PINEAPPLE PIZZAS

1 12" pre-baked pizza crust   1 package Alfredo sauce mix
12 slices precooked bacon   1 8 oz can pineapple tidbits
½ cup finely grated Cheddar cheese

Using a 2" biscuit cutter or a knife, cut rounds out of the pizza crust and put the rounds onto a baking
sheet. Make the Alfredo sauce according to the package directions. Chop the bacon.

Top each pizza crust round with 1 ½ teaspoons of sauce. Sprinkle lightly with the grated cheese. Divide
the precooked bacon and the pineapple tidbits over the pizza rounds. Sprinkle with any remaining cheese.
Bake at 350 for 12 to 15 minutes until bubbly.

NOTE: Chopped canned ham may be substituted for the precooked bacon.
NOTE: The pizza crusts may be either the commercial pre-baked type or home made (See Bread).
NOTE: This may also be made as a 12" pizza.

BACON PIE

14 slices precooked bacon, crumbled   1 cup grated Cheddar cheese
½ cup grated onion   2 cups milk made from dry
4 eggs, beaten   1 cup baking mix
½ teaspoon chicken bouillon granules   ½ teaspoon pepper

Coat a 10" pie plate with cooking spray. Sprinkle in the crumbled bacon, cheese, and onion. Beat the
remaining ingredients well and pour over the bacon. Bake at 350 for 45 to 55 minutes, until set and a
toothpick inserted into the middle comes out clean. Let stand for 5 minutes before cutting.

BACON QUICHE

1 unbaked pie crust

½ teaspoon salt

½ cup evaporated milk

2 teaspoons dried chives

½ cup grated Cheddar cheese

6 eggs

½ teaspoon pepper

1 4 oz can sliced mushrooms, drained

10 slices precooked bacon

Put the pie crust into a 9" or a 10" pie plate. Whisk the eggs, spices, and milk together. Dice the precooked bacon and stir in. Stir in the mushrooms and the cheese. Pour into the pie crust and bake at 350 for 30 to 40 minutes until a toothpick put in the middle comes out clean.

NOTE: This quiche may be made without any crust if desired. Pour into a pie plate that has been coated with cooking spray.

GRILLED BACON AND CHEESE SANDWICHES

4 slices bread

4 thin slices Cheddar cheese

8 slices precooked bacon

Butter

Coat 2 slices of the bread with softened butter and place buttered side down in a hot skillet. Remove from the heat while you top each slice of the bread with 1 piece of the cheese, 4 slices of the bacon, and another slice of cheese. Coat the remaining bread slices with butter and put on the sandwiches butter side up. Return to the heat and brown the sandwiches on both sides.

PASTA WITH BACON AND VEGETABLES

2 cups raw corkscrew pasta

½ cup chopped onion

1 teaspoon garlic powder

1 teaspoon dried parsley flakes

½ cup milk made from dry

14 slices precooked bacon, crumbled

1 chicken bouillon cube

1 tablespoon oil

½ teaspoon dried basil, crumbled

1 can cream of chicken soup

1 can mixed vegetables, drained

Cook the pasta in boiling water with the bouillon cube. Sauté the onion in the oil for 2 minutes until tender. Mix the soup, milk, and spices. Combine all ingredients and cook over medium heat for 10 minutes until heated through, stirring frequently.

CHILI

CHILI MAC IN A BOWL

2 cans chili without beans
2 teaspoons chili powder
1 can chili beans, not drained

3 cups water
1 cup cooked macaroni

Combine all ingredients and cook over medium heat for 10 minutes.

CHILI POT PIE

2 cans chili with or without beans
1 cup self rising flour
1 cup milk made from dry

½ cup water
½ cup melted butter

Mix the chili with the water and put into a baking dish that has been coated with cooking spray. Mix the flour, butter, and milk and pour the mixture over the chili. Bake at 350 for 45 minutes until the crust is browned.

CHILI SHEPHERD'S PIE

1 package instant mashed potato flakes
½ cup water
½ cup grated Cheddar cheese

2 cans chili without beans
1 can kidney beans, drained

Prepare the instant mashed potatoes as directed on the package. Mix the chili, water, and beans together and pour into a baking dish which has been coated with cooking spray. Top with the prepared potatoes, leveling them out evenly over the chili mixture. Bake at 350 for 30 to 35 minutes until the potatoes begin to lightly brown. Sprinkle with the cheese and bake for 5 more minutes.

CHILI TOPPED SPAGHETTI

1 can of chili without beans
1 teaspoon chili powder
¼ cup finely chopped onions

¾ cup water
3 cups cooked spaghetti
¼ cup grated Cheddar cheese

Combine the chili, water, and chili powder. Cook 5 minutes over medium heat. Top each serving of the spaghetti with the chili, onions, and cheese.

CHUCKWAGON STEW

2 cans chili with beans	3 cups water
1 can mixed vegetables, drained	2 teaspoons chili powder

Combine all ingredients and cook over medium heat for 10 minutes.

CORNED BEEF

CORNED BEEF DINNER

1 12 oz can corned beef	1 can whole potatoes, drained
1 can sauerkraut	1 can crinkle cut carrots, drained

Squeeze the moisture out of the sauerkraut and put into one forth of a baking dish that has been coated with cooking spray. Put the corned beef into one forth of the dish. Put in the potatoes, then the carrots. Bake at 350 for 30 minutes.

CORNED BEEF HASH

1 12 oz can corned beef	1 tablespoon oil
¼ cup chopped onion	1 can whole potatoes, drained
1 teaspoon pepper	2 eggs, optional

Sauté the onion in the oil for 2 minutes until tender. Dice the corned beef and the potatoes and add to the skillet. Sprinkle with the pepper. Cook over high heat, stirring frequently, until the potatoes begin to brown. If desired, fry the eggs and put on top of the hash.

CORNED BEEF SALAD

1 12 oz can corned beef	1 can whole potatoes, drained
¼ cup mayonnaise	¼ cup prepared 1,000 Island dressing
¼ cup finely chopped onion	

Cut the corned beef and potatoes into ½" cubes. Mix the mayonnaise, dressing, and onion and stir into the corned beef. Chill before serving.

CORNED BEEF SANDWICH

4 slices of canned corned beef

2 slices Cheddar cheese

4 slices bread

½ cup canned sauerkraut

2 tablespoons prepared 1,000 Island dressing

Squeeze the liquid out of the sauerkraut. Layer each slice of bread with 2 slices of the corned beef, half of the sauerkraut, the dressing, then the cheese. Put the remaining slices of bread on top.

REUBEN CASSEROLE

1 12 oz can corned beef

1 can whole potatoes, drained

½ cup prepared 1,000 Island dressing

1 can sauerkraut

1 cup grated Cheddar cheese

Cut the corned beef and potatoes into ½" cubes. Squeeze the moisture out of the sauerkraut.. Layer the corned beef and potatoes into a baking dish that has been coated with cooking spray. Cover the corned beef layer with the sauerkraut. Sprinkle with the cheese. Top with the dressing. Bake at 350 for 30 minutes.

PEPPERONI

PEPPERONI PASTA SALAD

1 ½ cups raw penne pasta

1 4 oz package sliced pepperoni, diced

½ teaspoon dried basil, crumbled

½ teaspoon Italian spices

½ cup prepared Italian salad dressing

1 chicken bouillon cube

1 cup Cheddar Cheese, diced

½ teaspoon pepper

¼ cup grated Parmesan cheese

¼ cup prepared ranch salad dressing

Cook the pasta in boiling water with the bouillon cube. Cool. Dice the pepperoni and the cheese. Mix the salad dressings and spices together. Mix all ingredients and stir. Chill before serving.

PEPPERONI PIE

CRUST:

½ cup chopped onion

1½ cups milk made from dry

¾ cup baking mix

½ teaspoon Italian seasoning

1/3 cup grated Parmesan cheese

3 eggs, beaten

½ teaspoon garlic powder

Coat a 10" pie plate with cooking spray. Sprinkle the onions and the Parmesan cheese over the bottom. Beat the milk, baking mix, eggs, and spices for 1 minute and pour into the pie plate. Bake at 350 for 20 minutes.

TOPPING:

1 cup tomato sauce

½ teaspoon Italian seasoning

½ cup chopped onion

1 cup grated Cheddar cheese

½ teaspoon garlic powder

¼ cup grated Parmesan cheese

1 4 oz package sliced pepperoni

Mix the tomato sauce and the spices and spread over the top of the baked crust. Layer on the remaining ingredients. Bake at 350 for an additional 15 minutes. Allow to set for 5 minutes before cutting.

PEPPERONI PIZZAS

1 12" pre-baked pizza crust

1 teaspoon garlic powder

3 slices of pepperoni for each pizza

1 8 oz can tomato sauce

½ cup grated Cheddar cheese

Using a 2" biscuit cutter or a knife, cut rounds out of the pizza crust and put the rounds onto a baking sheet. Stir the garlic powder into the tomato sauce. Top each pizza round with 2 teaspoons of the sauce. Divide the cheese over the pizzas. Top with the pepperoni. Bake at 350 for 12 to 15 minutes until bubbly.

NOTE: Other toppings such as black olives, sliced green olives, canned mushroom slices, or jalapeno pepper slices may be added.

NOTE: The pizza crusts may be either the commercial pre-baked type or home made (See Bread).

NOTE: This may also be made as a 12" pizza.

PEPPERONI QUESADILLAS

1 4 oz package sliced pepperoni
¼ cup grated Cheddar cheese

¼ cup salsa
4 flour tortillas

Divide the salsa, pepperoni, and cheese over 2 of the tortillas. Top with the remaining 2 tortillas. Cook each in a skillet until lightly browned on both sides. Cut each into 8 wedges to serve.

PEPPY MACARONI CASSEROLE

1 7 to 8 oz package macaroni and cheese
½ teaspoon garlic powder
1 8 oz can tomato sauce
1 cup grated Cheddar cheese

2 eggs, beaten
1 teaspoon Italian seasoning
½ cup diced pepperoni slices

Prepare the macaroni and cheese as directed on the box. Beat the eggs and fold into the macaroni. Pour into a 13 X 9 baking dish that has been coated with cooking spray. Mix the tomato sauce and the spices. Pour over the macaroni. Top with the diced pepperoni, then the cheese. Bake at 350 for 30 minutes. Let the casserole stand for 5 minutes to firm up before serving.

PIZZA CASSEROLE

1 8 oz package sliced pepperoni
1 chicken bouillon cube
1 8 oz can tomato sauce
½ teaspoon onion powder
1 4 oz can black olives, drained

1 8 oz package noodles
1 teaspoon Italian seasoning
½ teaspoon garlic powder
1 cup grated Cheddar cheese

Cook the noodles in boiling water with the bouillon cube. Drain well. Layer the noodles in a 9" baking dish that has been coated with cooking spray. Cover with the pepperoni slices and the black olives. Mix the tomato sauce, the seasonings, and the cheese and pour over the pepperoni layer. Bake at 350 for 30 minutes.

PORK ROAST

OPEN FACE ROAST PORK SANDWICHES

1 16 oz can roast pork and gravy
1 package instant mashed potato flakes

1 package pork gravy mix
4 slices of bread

Prepare the gravy mix as directed on the package. Prepare the mashed potatoes as directed on the package. Heat the roast pork and break up the pieces. Put 1 to 2 slices of bread on a plate. Top with part of the pork, then a scoop of the mashed potatoes, then the gravy.

PORK AND BEANS

1 16 oz can roast pork and gravy
½ teaspoon garlic powder
½ teaspoon chili powder
1 4 ½ oz can chopped green chilies, drained

1 can pinto beans, rinsed and drained
½ teaspoon ground cumin
½ teaspoon pepper
Tortillas

Combine the pork, beans, chilies, and spices. Bring to a boil. Reduce the heat and simmer for 5 minutes. Wrap portions of the mixture in the tortillas to serve.

PORK AND STUFFING

1 16 oz can roast pork and gravy
1 8 oz can crushed pineapple

1 6 oz box cornbread stuffing mix

Separate the pieces of pork into bite sized pieces and put into the bottom of a baking dish that has been coated with cooking spray. Prepare the stuffing mix as directed on the box, substituting the pineapple juice for part of the liquid. Stir the pineapple into the stuffing. Put the stuffing over the pork and bake at 350 for 30 minutes.

PORK AND SWEET POTATOES

1 16 oz can roast pork and gravy
1 8 oz can pineapple tidbits

1 20 oz can sweet potatoes, drained

Put the roast pork into half of a baking dish that has been coated with cooking spray. Put the sweet potatoes into the other half of the dish. Pour the pineapple and juice over the sweet potatoes. Bake at 360 for 20 to 25 minutes until bubbly.

PORK BBQ

2 16 oz cans roast pork and gravy   ¾ cup prepared BBQ sauce
¼ teaspoon hickory smoke flavoring

Drain the gravy from the pork. Save the gravy for another use. Combine all ingredients and bring to a boil. Reduce the heat to low and simmer for 10 minutes, stirring frequently. Serve on buns as a BBQ sandwich or mounded on a plate with chopped pickles and chopped onions.

PORK ROAST AND VEGETABLES

1 16 oz can roast pork and gravy   1 package pork gravy mix
1 can whole potatoes, drained   1 can whole carrots, drained

Put the potatoes into one third of a baking dish that has been coated with cooking spray. Put the carrots into another third of the dish. Put the pork into the rest of the dish. Prepare the gravy mix as directed on the package. Pour over the pork and vegetables. Bake at 350 for 30 minutes until bubbly.

PORK ROAST WITH DRIED FRUIT

1 16 oz can roast pork and gravy   1 package pork gravy mix
1 cup mixed dried fruit

Prepare the gravy mix as directed on the package. Put the pork and dried fruit into a baking dish that has been coated with cooking spray. Pour the gravy mix over the pork. Bake at 350 for 30 minutes until the dried fruit is tender.

PORK STEW

1 16 oz can roast pork and gravy   1 package pork gravy mix
1 can diced tomatoes   1 can whole potatoes, drained
1 can peas and carrots, drained   1 teaspoon dried chives
2 cups water   1 teaspoon pepper

Combine the water, tomatoes, and gravy mix and bring to a boil. Dice the potatoes. Add the remaining ingredients and bring back to a boil. Reduce the heat to medium and cook for 15 minutes.

PORK WITH SAUERKRAUT

1 16 oz can roast pork and gravy
1 can whole potatoes, drained

1 can sauerkraut, drained
1 can crinkle cut carrots, drained

Put the pork into one fourth of a baking dish that has been coated with cooking spray. Squeeze the liquid out of the sauerkraut and put it into one fourth of the dish. Repeat with the potatoes and the carrots. Bake at 350 for 30 minutes.

SPICY PORK

2 16 oz cans roast pork and gravy
1 cup water
1 4 oz can chopped green chilies, drained

1 package taco seasoning mix
½ teaspoon garlic powder
Tortillas

Combine the pork, seasoning mix, water, chilies, and garlic. Bring to a boil. Reduce the heat to medium and cook for 10 minutes. Put a small amount into the tortillas and roll to serve.

SUMMER SAUSAGE

SAUSAGE BEER SOUP

¼ cup butter, divided
½ cup all purpose flour
½ cup milk made from dry
1 can whole potatoes
1½ teaspoon Worcestershire sauce
1 ½ cups grated Cheddar cheese

½ cup chopped onion
1 can chicken broth
½ cup beer
½ teaspoon garlic powder
½ teaspoon dry mustard
8 summer sausage slices, sliced ¼" thick

Cut the summer sausage slices into bite sized pieces and fry for 1 to 2 minutes. Remove from the skillet and blot the oil. Wipe the skillet out with paper towels and melt 2 tablespoons of the butter. Sauté the onion in the butter for 2 minutes until tender. Dice the potatoes. Remove the onions from the skillet. Melt the remaining 2 tablespoons of butter and stir in the flour. Whisk until smooth and slowly whisk in the chicken broth. When that mixture is smooth, stir in the beer and the milk. Add the potatoes and the onions, the seasonings, and the cheese. Cook over medium heat until the cheese melts, stirring constantly and not letting the mixture boil. Sprinkle the summer sausage over each bowl of the soup.

SUMMER SAUSAGE FRIED RICE

½ cup summer sausage, diced
¼ cup chopped onion
2 cups water
1 can tomatoes with green chilies
1 cup uncooked rice

1 tablespoon oil
½ teaspoon garlic powder
2 ½ teaspoons chicken bouillon granules
½ cup canned peas and carrots, drained

Sauté the summer sausage for 2 minutes, stirring frequently, until beginning to brown. Remove from the skillet and blot with paper towels. Wipe the skillet and sauté the onions in the oil for 2 minutes until tender. Stir in the rice and sauté for 2 minutes. Mix the water, bouillon, and the tomatoes. Cover and simmer for 15 to 20 minutes until the liquid is absorbed. Stir in the diced summer sausage and the peas and carrots.

SUMMER SAUSAGE QUESADILLA

For each quesadilla:
1 flour or corn tortilla
2 tablespoons refried beans
1 tablespoon grated Cheddar cheese

2 slices summer sausage, ¼" thick
2 tablespoons salsa

Dice the summer sausage and fry for 1 minutes. Blot off the oil. Drain the liquid from the salsa. Mix the salsa into the refried beans and spread the mixture one half of the tortilla. Top with the sausage and the cheese. Fold the tortilla in half and put into a skillet. Toast each side for 1 to 2 minutes until very lightly browned.

SUMMER SAUSAGE REUBEN

For each sandwich:
2 slices bread
2 tablespoons canned sauerkraut, well drained
1 tablespoon prepared Thousand Island dressing

4 slices summer sausage ¼" thick
1 slice Cheddar cheese
Butter for toasting

Fry the summer sausage slices for 1 minute per side and blot off the oil. Spread one side of each piece of bread with softened butter. On the side that has not been buttered, spread 1 teaspoon of the dressing. Top with the sausage slices, the sauerkraut, the cheese slice and the remaining 2 teaspoons of dressing. Put the second piece of bread onto the sandwich and toast until each side is browned.

SUMMER SAUSAGE WITH MUSHROOMS

¾ cup summer sausage, diced

1 8 oz can tomato sauce

¼ teaspoon onion powder

½ teaspoon pepper

Hot cooked rice

1 4 oz can sliced mushrooms, drained

¼ teaspoon garlic powder

1 teaspoon dried chives

¼ cup water

Sauté the summer sausage for 2 minutes until it begins to brown. Remove from the skillet and blot with paper towels. Mix the sausage, mushrooms, sauce, water, and spices. Bring to a boil and reduce the heat. Simmer for 5 minutes. Serve over the rice.

PIES, COBBLERS, CRISPS

Almost Apple Pie

Applesauce Pie

Chess Pie

Chocolate Chess Pie

Chocolate Pie

Easiest Pie Crust Ever

Easy Fruit Cobbler

Easy Fruit Crisp

Graham Cracker Pie Crust

Magic Coconut Pie

Pie Crust

Pineapple Coconut Pie

Pumpkin Pie

Raisin Crunch Pie

Saltine Cracker Pie Crust

ALMOST APPLE PIE

1 unbaked pie crust

2 teaspoons cream of tartar

22 round buttery crackers

1 teaspoon ground cinnamon

1 ½ cups sugar

1 2/3 cups hot water

2 tablespoons butter

Put the pie crust into a 9" pie plate and bake at 350 for 5 minutes. Mix the water, sugar, and cream of tartar together and boil for 2 minutes. Add the crackers and boil for 2 more minutes. Remove from the heat and add the butter and the cinnamon. Pour into the pie crust and bake at 450 for 15 minutes until browned.

APPLESAUCE PIE

1 unbaked pie crust

3 tablespoons lemon juice from bottle

4 eggs, beaten

½ teaspoon salt

1 cup applesauce

¾ cup sugar

2 tablespoons butter, softened

Beat the eggs and the sugar. Beat in the butter, applesauce, lemon juice, and salt. Pour into the pie crust and bake at 350 for 35 to 40 minutes until the center is set.

CHESS PIE

1 unbaked pie crust

1¼ cups sugar

1½ teaspoons white vinegar

½ cup softened butter

3 eggs

1 ½ teaspoons corn meal

Beat the sugar, meal, and butter together. Beat in the eggs and the vinegar. Pour into the pie crust and bake at 350 for 30 to 35 minutes and the pie is set.

CHOCOLATE CHESS PIE

Unbaked pie crust

2 eggs

¼ cup butter, softened

3 tablespoons cocoa powder

1 ¼ cups sugar

3 tablespoons corn starch

¼ cup evaporated milk

1 teaspoon vanilla

Mix the dry ingredients together. Beat the eggs and butter together. Beat in the milk. Stir in the vanilla and the dry ingredients. Pour into an unbaked pie crust and bake at 325 for 40 minutes until the center is set.

CHOCOLATE PIE

2 eggs, beaten

1 cup butter, melted and cooled

½ cup all purpose flour

½ cup sugar

½ cup brown sugar

1 6 oz bag chocolate chips

1 cup walnuts, chopped

1 unbaked pie crust

Beat the eggs until foamy. Add the flour and sugars and beat until well blended. Blend in the butter. Stir in the chocolate chips and the nuts. Pour into the pie crust and bake at 325 for 1 hour.

NOTE: This is good with peanut butter chips.

EASIEST PIE CRUST EVER

1 ½ cups all purpose flour

1 teaspoon salt

½ cup canola or vegetable oil

2 tablespoons water

Mix all ingredients until a ball is formed. Press evenly into a pie plate and bake 350 for 12 to 18 minutes until it just begins to brown.

EASY FRUIT COBBLER

1 28 oz can peaches, apricots, or fruit cocktail

1 cup baking mix

1/3 cup milk made from dry

¼ teaspoon cinnamon

½ teaspoon vanilla

Drain the fruit well. Dice the large pieces of fruit and put into a baking dish which has been coated with cooking spray. Mix the remaining ingredients and pour over the fruit. Bake at 350 for 30 to 35 minutes.

EASY FRUIT CRISP

1 can pie filling, your choice of flavor   1 single layer size box cake mix
½ cup melted butter   ¼ cup chopped nuts

Spread the pie filling evenly in a small baking dish which has been coated with cooking spray. Combine the cake mix, butter, and nuts. Sprinkle the cake mix over the pie filling. Bake at 350 for 35 to 40 minutes until the topping is lightly browned.

GRAHAM CRACKER PIE CRUST

1 ½ cups graham cracker crumbs   2 tablespoons sugar or sweetener
¼ cup melted butter

Mix the crumbs and the sugar in the pie plate. Drizzle the butter over the crumbs and mix thoroughly. Press very firmly on the bottom and sides of the pie plate. Bake at 350 for 8 minutes. Cool before filling.

MAGIC COCONUT PIE

¼ cup self rising flour or baking mix   ¾ cup sugar or sweetener
2 eggs   1 cup milk made from dry
½ cup softened butter   1 teaspoon vanilla
1 cup flaked coconut   1 can Mandarin oranges, drained

Beat the eggs well. Mix in the sugar and the flour. Beat in the butter, milk, vanilla, and coconut. Mix well. Pour into a pie plate which has been coated with cooking spray. Bake at 350 for 30 to 35 minutes. When serving, top the pie with the Mandarin oranges.

PIE CRUST

1 ¼ cups all purpose flour   ½ teaspoon salt
1/3 cup solid shortening   3 to 4 tablespoons ice water

Cut the shortening into the flour and salt with a pastry cutter or two kitchen knives until it resembles coarse meal. Sprinkle with 3 tablespoons of the water and mix until it forms a ball. Add the additional water if needed. Roll out on a lightly floured board to a circle which will cover your pie pan. Press into the pie pan. If using as a pre baked crust, puncture the crust with the tines of a fork every 1 to 1 ½ inches. Bake at 350 for 12 to 18 minutes until just beginning to brown.

PINEAPPLE COCONUT PIE

6 tablespoons butter, melted

3 tablespoons all purpose flour

1 cup canned crushed pineapple, drained

1 unbaked pie crust

3 eggs

1 ¼ cups sugar

1 cup flaked coconut

Combine the butter, eggs, flour, and sugar and beat until blended. Stir in the pineapple and the coconut and pour into the pie crust. Bake at 350 for 45 to 55 minutes until the filling is set.

PUMPKIN PIE

1 unbaked pie crust

1 can sweetened condensed milk

¾ teaspoon ground cinnamon

1 15 oz can pumpkin

2 eggs

½ teaspoon salt

Beat the pumpkin, condensed milk, eggs, cinnamon, and salt together and pour into the pie crust. Bake at 400 for 15 minutes, lower the heat to 350 and bake 40 more minutes until the center is set and a toothpick inserted into the center comes out clean.

RAISIN CRUNCH PIE

2 eggs, beaten

½ cup flaked coconut

¾ cup sugar

1 teaspoon vanilla

½ cup butter, softened

½ cup chopped pecans or walnuts

½ cup raisins

1 unbaked pie crust.

Beat all ingredients and pour into the pie crust. Bake at 300 for 55 minutes.

SALTINE CRACKER PIE CRUST

24 saltine cracker squares   ¼ cup butter

Finely crush the saltines. Melt the butter and mix with the crumbs. Firmly press into the bottom of a 9"
pie plate. Pour in your choice of filling and bake as directed for the filling. This is especially good as the
base of a quiche.

ROAST BEEF AND DRIED BEEF

BBQ Shredded Beef

Beef and Bean Roll

Beef and Bean Tostadas

Beef and Noodle Casserole

Beef and Vegetable Bake

Beef and Vegetable Casserole

Beef and Vegetable Skillet

Beef Enchiladas

Beef Goulash

Beef over Rice

Beef Pot Pie

Beef Roast and Vegetables

Burrito Bake

Chili Rellenos Casserole

Chili Mac

Creamed Dried Beef

Dried Beef Casserole

Italian Beef

Mexican Shepherd's Pie

Microwave Mexican Casserole

One Pot Pasta

Open Faced Roast Beef Sandwiches

Pasta Beef Bake

Pepper Steak

Shepherd's Pie

Spicy Hash

Texas Hash

BBQ SHREDDED BEEF

2 16 oz cans roast beef with gravy

1 teaspoon hickory smoke flavoring

½ teaspoon onion powder

1 cup prepared BBQ sauce

½ teaspoon garlic powder

2 drops hot sauce

Drain the roast beef well and shred. Mix all ingredients and bring to a boil. Reduce the heat and simmer for 15 minutes, stirring frequently. Serve as BBQ sandwiches.

BEEF AND BEAN ROLL

1 16 oz can roast beef and gravy

1 4 oz can chopped green chilies, drained

1 cup salsa

8 flour tortillas

1 16 oz can refried beans

1 package taco seasoning mix

1 cup grated Cheddar cheese

Dice the roast beef and stir in the taco seasoning mix. Add the chilies, refried beans, and the salsa and simmer for 10 minutes. Divide the cheese among the tortillas. Top with the beef mixture. Roll up and microwave for 2 to 3 minutes.

BEEF AND BEAN TOSTADAS

4 corn tortillas

1 7 oz can of roast beef, drained

½ teaspoon garlic powder

½ teaspoon cumin

½ cup grated Cheddar cheese

¼ cup oil

1 can red beans, rinsed and drained

½ teaspoon chili powder

1 teaspoon lime juice from bottle

¼ cup prepared salsa or taco sauce

Put the oil into a skillet and fry the corn tortillas one at a time for 2 minutes on each side until crispy. Drain on paper towels. Combine the beef, beans, spices, and lime juice and divide the mixture over the tostadas. Sprinkle with the cheese. Top each tostada with 1 tablespoon of the salsa.

BEEF AND NOODLE CASSEROLE

8 oz noodles

1 16 oz can beef with gravy

1 4 oz can sliced mushrooms, drained

1 beef bouillon cube

1 can beef gravy

salt, pepper to taste

Cook the noodles in boiling water with the beef bouillon cube. Drain well. Stir the beef, gravy, mushrooms, salt, and pepper together. Add to the noodle mixture. Pour into a baking dish and bake at 350 for 30 minutes, stirring after 15 minutes.

BEEF AND VEGETABLE BAKE

1 16 oz can roast beef and gravy
½ cup grated Cheddar cheese
1½ cups milk made from dry
1 teaspoon paprika
½ teaspoon pepper

1 can mixed vegetables, drained
½ cup baking mix
2 teaspoons spicy mustard
½ teaspoon dried parsley flakes
2 eggs, beaten

Cut the roast beef into bite sized pieces. Mix the beef and the vegetables. Beat the remaining ingredients together and combine with the beef. Pour into a baking dish that has been coated with cooking spray. Bake at 350 for 45 minutes.

BEEF AND VEGETABLE CASSEROLE

1 16 oz can roast beef and gravy
1 can cream of mushroom soup
1 2 oz can chow mein noodles

1 can mixed vegetables, drained
1 can chicken and rice soup

Dice the roast beef. Mix all ingredients and pour into a baking dish that has been coated with cooking spray. Bake at 350 for 45 minutes until bubbly.

BEEF AND VEGETABLE SKILLET

1 16 oz can roast beef and gravy
¼ cup water
¼ teaspoon garlic powder

1 can mixed vegetables, drained
2 teaspoons soy sauce
½ teaspoon dried chives

Shred the beef and mix with the remaining ingredients. Bring to a boil, reduce the heat and simmer for 5 minutes.

BEEF ENCHILLADAS

1 16 oz can roast beef and gravy

1 tablespoon chili powder

1 4 ½ oz can chopped green chilies, drained

6 flour tortillas

¼ cup additional grated Cheddar cheese

¼ cup chopped onion

¼ teaspoon cumin

½ cup grated Cheddar cheese

1 10 oz can enchilada sauce

1 4 oz can black olives, drained

Drain the roast beef and shred. Stir the onion, drained gravy, and spices into the beef. Divide the mixture among tortillas. Divide the ½ cup of cheese among the tortillas. Roll and put into a baking dish that has been coated with cooking spray. Pour the enchilada sauce over and bake at 350 for 20 minutes. Sprinkle the ¼ cup of cheese over and top with the olives. Bake an additional 5 minutes.

BEEF GOULASH

2 cans sliced mushrooms, drained

2 tablespoons oil, divided

1 cup onions cut into strips

2 tablespoons Worcestershire sauce

1 teaspoon garlic powder

1 16 oz can roast beef with gravy

2 tablespoons flour

1 cup beef broth

2 teaspoons paprika

Hot cooked noodles

Drain the gravy from the beef and reserve the gravy. Sauté the onion strips in 1 tablespoon of the oil for 2 to 3 minutes until tender. Remove the onions from the skillet and coat with the remaining oil. Spread the beef evenly into the skillet. Sprinkle with the flour and stir gently. Sauté for 4 to 5 minutes before turning and repeating. Return the onions to the skillet. Mix the beef broth and spices and pour over the beef. Heat for 8 to 10 minutes until bubbly. Serve over hot noodles.

NOTE: 1 cup of water and 2 beef bouillon cubes may be substituted for the beef broth.

BEEF OVER RICE

1 16 oz can roast beef

1 can cream of mushroom soup

Salt, pepper to taste

Dried parsley flakes

1 4 oz can sliced mushrooms, drained

1 teaspoon Worcestershire sauce

2 cups cooked rice

Mix the beef, mushrooms, soup, Worcestershire sauce, salt, and pepper. Cook over medium heat for 10 minutes until heated through. Serve over the rice and sprinkle with the parsley flakes.

BEEF POT PIE

1 cup self rising flour

1 cup milk made from dry

1 can peas and carrots, drained

1 can cream of chicken soup

½ cup melted butter

1 16 oz can roast beef and gravy

1 can whole potatoes, drained

Mix the flour, melted butter, and milk. Dice the potatoes. Mix the potatoes, beef, vegetables, and soup. Pour into a pie plate that has been coated with cooking spray. Pour the flour batter over the beef mixture. Put the pie plate on a baking tray that has been lined with aluminum foil to catch any drips as the pie bakes. Bake at 350 for 35 to 45 minutes until the top crust is lightly browned.

NOTE: 2 cans of mixed vegetables, drained, may be substituted for the peas, carrots, and potatoes.

BEEF ROAST AND VEGETABLES

1 16 oz can roast beef and gravy

1 can whole potatoes, drained

1 package beef gravy mix

1 can whole carrots, drained

Put the potatoes into one third of a baking dish that has been coated with cooking spray. Put the carrots into another third of the dish. Put the beef into the rest of the dish. Prepare the gravy mix as directed on the package. Pour over the beef and vegetables. Bake at 350 for 30 minutes until bubbly.

BURRITO BAKE

1 16 oz can roast beef and gravy

1 can refried beans

1 cup baking mix

1 cup salsa

1 cup grated Cheddar cheese

¼ cup water

Dice the beef. Mix the refried beans, water, and baking mix and press into a lightly greased pie plate. Spread the diced beef evenly over the crust. Cover with the salsa, then the cheese. Bake at 350 for 30 minutes. Serve with tortilla chips (See Bread).

CHILE RELLENOS CASSEROLE

2 cans whole green chilies

2 teaspoons chili powder

½ teaspoon onion powder

2 tablespoons all purpose flour

½ teaspoon salt

2 cups grated Cheddar cheese

1 6 oz can roast beef with gravy

½ teaspoon garlic powder

¼ cup milk made from dry

3 eggs

½ teaspoon pepper

Drain the green chilies well and cut in half lengthwise. Spread the chilies to cover the bottom of a baking dish which has been coated with cooking spray. Drain the roast beef and shred. Mix with the dry seasonings. Spread the beef mixture evenly over the chilies. Sprinkle with the cheese. Mix the eggs, milk, and flour until smooth. Gently pour over the beef. Bake uncovered at 350 for 30 to 35 minutes until set.

CHILI MAC

1 16 oz can roast beef and gravy

1 tablespoon oil

1 teaspoon garlic powder

Salt, pepper to taste

½ cup grated Cheddar cheese

½ cup chopped onion

1 can diced tomatoes

1 tablespoon chili powder

½ cup raw macaroni

Corn chips and additional cheese

Drain the roast beef and chop. Sauté the onion in the oil for 2 minutes until tender. Cook the macaroni in boiling and salted water until done. Combine the cooked macaroni, beef, onion, spices, and tomatoes. Pour into a baking dish that has been coated with cooking spray. Bake at 350 for 20 to 25 minutes until bubbly. Sprinkle with the cheese and bake 5 more minutes. Serve over broken corn chips and topped with cheese.

NOTE: This may also be cooked on the stove over medium heat for 20 minutes, stirring frequently.

CREAMED DRIED BEEF

1 5 oz jar dried beef

2 tablespoons flour

1 teaspoon Worcestershire sauce

1 4 oz can sliced mushrooms, drained

2 tablespoons butter

1 cup evaporated milk

½ cup canned peas, drained

¼ teaspoon pepper

Shred the dried beef. Melt the butter and whisk in the flour. Cook 2 minutes, stirring constantly. Slowly add the milk, whisking well. Stir in the Worcestershire sauce and the pepper. Cook over medium heat for 5 minutes until it begins to thicken. Stir in the mushrooms, peas, and pepper. Heat 5 more minutes.

NOTE: This may be served over toast, mashed potatoes, rice, or noodles.

DRIED BEEF CASSEROLE

1 cup evaporated milk
2 hard boiled eggs
¼ cup diced onion
1 5 oz jar dried beef

1 can cream of celery soup
1 cup raw macaroni
1 cup grated Cheddar cheese

Mix all ingredients and refrigerate at least 3 hours before baking. Let the casserole come to room temperature for 30 minutes. Bake at 350 for 35 minutes.

ITALIAN BEEF

2 16 oz cans roast beef with gravy
1 ½ teaspoons mustard seed
1 16 oz can Pepperoncini peppers, undrained

¼ cup Worcestershire sauce
2 packages dry Italian salad dressing mix
¼ cup water

Put all ingredients into a slow cooker and cook on low for 4 to 6 hours or on high for 2 to 3 hours. Serve as sandwiches or as a main dish meat.

MEXICAN SHEPHERD'S PIE

1 package instant mashed potato flakes
1 tablespoon oil
1 cup canned corn, drained
1 3 oz can sliced black olives, drained
2 teaspoons chili powder
Salt, pepper to taste

½ cup chopped onion
1 to 2 16 oz cans roast beef with gravy
1 can diced tomatoes, drained
1 package taco seasoning mix
½ teaspoon garlic powder
1 cup grated Cheddar cheese

Sauté the onion in the oil for 2 minutes until tender. Combine the onion, beef and gravy, corn, drained tomatoes, olives, and spices. Pour into a baking dish which has been coated with cooking spray. Prepare the potatoes as directed on the package and add the cheese. Stir until the cheese is melted. Spread evenly over the beef mixture. Bake at 350 for 20 to 25 minutes.

NOTE: This is better when made with 2 cans of roast beef but lighter when made with 1 can.

MICROWAVE MEXICAN CASSEROLE

1 16 oz can roast beef and gravy, drained
1 tablespoon oil
1 ½ teaspoons chili powder
1 can cream of mushroom soup
¾ cup evaporated milk
¾ cup grated Cheddar cheese

½ cup chopped onion
1 teaspoon garlic powder
1 4 ½ oz can chopped green chilies, drained
1 10 oz can enchilada sauce
3 cups tortilla chips, divided

Sauté the onion in the oil for 2 minutes until tender. Drain the roast beef and chop. Mix the beef, spices, chilies, soup, sauce, and milk. Put 2 cups coarsely broken tortilla chips into a baking dish that is microwave safe and that has been coated with cooking spray. Spoon half of the meat mixture over the chips. Cover with half of the cheese. Cover with the remaining tortilla chips and the remaining meat mixture. Cover with plastic wrap and fold back over one of the corners. Microwave on high for 10 to 12 minutes. Sprinkle with the remaining cheese and let set 5 minutes before serving.

ONE POT PASTA

½ cup chopped onion
1 16 oz can roast beef with gravy
1 teaspoon garlic powder
2 cans sliced mushrooms, drained
3 cups corkscrew pasta, not cooked
1 cup grated Cheddar cheese

1 tablespoon oil
1 26 to 28 oz can spaghetti sauce
1 teaspoon chili powder
3 cups water
Salt, pepper to taste

Sauté the onion in the oil for 2 minutes until tender. Shred and chop the beef. Mix the onion, beef, sauce, spices, mushrooms, and water together. Stir in the raw pasta. Bring the mixture to a boil. Reduce the heat, cover, and cook 20 minutes, stirring frequently. Check for doneness. Add the salt and pepper if needed. Sprinkle each serving with the grated cheese.

OPEN FACED ROAST BEEF SANDWICHES

1 package instant mashed potato flakes
1 can beef gravy

1 16 oz can roast beef and gravy
4 slices bread

Prepare the mashed potatoes according to the package directions. Heat the roast beef and the can of gravy. Serve the bread covered with the roast beef. Cover each serving with a generous spoonful of the mashed potatoes. Top with the remaining beef gravy.

NOTE: A package of brown gravy mix, prepared according to package directions, may be substituted for the can of gravy.

PASTA BEEF BAKE

2 cups various shapes of pasta
½ cup chopped onion
1 26 oz can spaghetti sauce with meat
1 cup grated Cheddar cheese
½ teaspoon basil

1 16 oz can roast beef and gravy
1 can sliced mushrooms, drained
1 egg, beaten
½ teaspoon garlic powder
1 teaspoon Italian spices

Cook the pasta in boiling, salted water as directed on the package. Dice the roast beef. Stir the pasta, beef, onion, mushrooms, sauce, spices, and egg together and put into an 8" baking dish that has been coated with cooking spray. Bake, uncovered, at 350 for 20 to 25 minutes until bubbly. Top with the cheese and bake another 5 minutes.

NOTE: This is a good way to use small amounts of your bowtie, penne, corkscrew, etc., pastas.

PEPPER STEAK

1 16 oz can roast beef and gravy
½ cup onion, sliced into rings
1 can sliced mushrooms, drained
½ teaspoon pepper
½ teaspoon garlic powder
1 beef bouillon cube
2 cups cooked rice

1 ½ tablespoons soy sauce
1 tablespoon oil
½ cup roasted red pepper from can
¼ teaspoon ground ginger
½ cup water
1 tablespoon corn starch

Dice the roast beef into bite sized pieces. Sauté the onion rings in the oil for 2 minutes until tender. Slice the roasted red pepper into match stick pieces. Mix the water, corn starch, and bouillon cube. Combine all ingredients and bring to the boiling point. Reduce the heat and simmer, uncovered, for 15 minutes. Serve over the rice.

NOTE: One 2 oz can diced and drained pimentos may be substituted for the roasted red pepper.

SHEPHERD'S PIE

1 package instant mashed potato flakes

1 can peas and carrots, drained

½ cup grated Cheddar cheese

1 to 2 16 oz cans roast beef with gravy

1 can sliced mushrooms, drained

Prepare the instant mashed potatoes as directed on the package. Mix all other ingredients together and pour into a baking dish which has been coated with cooking spray. Top with the prepared potatoes, leveling them out evenly over the beef mixture. Bake at 350 for 30 to 35 minutes until the potatoes begin to lightly brown. Sprinkle with the cheese and bake for 5 more minutes.

NOTE: This is better when made with 2 cans of roast beef but lighter when made with 1 can.

SPICY HASH

2 tablespoons butter or oil

1 16 oz can roast beef with gravy

1 can diced tomatoes with chilies

½ cup diced onion

1 can whole potatoes

salt, pepper to taste

Melt the butter in a skillet. Sauté the onion for 2 minutes until tender. Dice the can of potatoes and brown in the butter. Drain the gravy from the roast and save for another use. Dice the beef. Stir into the skillet and cook on high for 5 minutes, stirring frequently. Drain the juice from the tomatoes and stir the tomatoes into the mixture. Season to taste with the salt and pepper. Cook for 3 to 5 minutes until heated through.

NOTE: Traditionally, a fried egg will be served over the serving of hash.

TEXAS HASH

1 16 oz can roast beef and gravy

1 can diced tomatoes

2 teaspoons Worcestershire sauce

1 medium onion, sliced

1 ½ teaspoons chili powder

½ cup raw rice

Chop the roast beef. Combine all ingredients and put into a slow cooker. Cook on low for 6 to 8 hours or on high for 4 to 6 hours.

SALADS

Applesauce Salad

Bean Salad

Beet and Orange Salad

Black Bean, Rice, and Corn Salad

Black Bean Salad

Calico Salad

Corn Relish

Easy Pickled Beets

Holiday Salad

Marinated Artichokes

Marinated Vegetable Salad

Pea and Peanut Salad

Pea Salad

Pickled Onions

Pineapple Salad

APPLESAUCE SALAD

2 cups canned applesauce
1 cup lemon lime soda

1 package cherry gelatin mix

Heat the applesauce until it is nearly boiling. Dissolve the gelatin in the hot mixture. Add the soda and mix well. Refrigerate until firm before serving.

BEAN SALAD

1 can green beans, drained
1 can black beans, rinsed and drained
½ cup prepared Italian dressing

1 can yellow beans, drained
1 can cut baby corn, drained

Mix the drained vegetables and chill. Mix in the Italian dressing just before serving.

NOTE: Instead of the yellow beans, another can of green beans or a can of rinsed and drained kidney beans may be used.
NOTE: Individual servings of the vegetables may be taken out and mixed with the dressing.

BEET AND ORANGE SALAD

4 tablespoons water
2 ½ tablespoons canola oil
1 ½ teaspoons sugar
2 cans Mandarin oranges, drained

¼ teaspoon orange flavoring
1 tablespoon lemon juice
salt, pepper to taste
2 cans sliced beets, rinsed and drained

Combine the water, flavoring, oil, sugar, lemon juice, salt, and pepper. Mix well. Layer the beets and the orange sections. Pour the dressing over and lightly mix. Chill.

BLACK BEAN, RICE, AND CORN SALAD

1 ½ cups cooked rice
2 tablespoons olive or canola oil
1 can black beans, rinsed and drained
2 teaspoons dried cilantro

6 tablespoons lemon juice
1/2 teaspoon garlic powder
1 cup canned corn, drained
2 teaspoons chili powder

Combine all ingredients and mix well. Let stand until cool. Serve chilled or at room temperature.

BLACK BEAN SALAD

½ cup chopped onion
1 can black beans, rinsed and drained
1 tablespoon lime juice from bottle

1 can corn, drained
1/3 cup prepared Italian salad dressing

Combine the onion, corn, and black beans. Mix the salad dressing and the lime juice. Pour over the bean mixture and mix well.

CALICO SALAD

1 can yellow corn, drained
1 can sliced water chestnuts, drained
1 2 oz jar pimientos, drained and chopped
1/3 cup Parmesan cheese
1 tablespoon lemon juice
½ cup slivered almonds, toasted (optional)

1 can peas, drained
¼ cup chopped onion
½ cup mayonnaise
¼ cup milk made from dry
½ teaspoon salt

Combine the corn, peas, water chestnuts, onions, and pimientos. Mix the mayonnaise, cheese, milk, lemon juice, and salt. Pour over the vegetables and stir to coat. Cover and refrigerate for at least 2 hours. Top with the toasted almonds just before serving.

CORN RELISH

1 cup sugar
1 teaspoon celery seed
1 cup vinegar
2 cans corn, not drained

1 teaspoon salt
1/2 teaspoon dry mustard
2 tablespoons minced dry onion flakes
2 tablespoons chopped pimiento

Heat the sugar, salt, celery seed, dry mustard, and vinegar to boiling. Boil 2 minutes. Stir in the corn and the remaining ingredients. Cool and refrigerate at least 3 days to develop the flavor.

EASY PICKLED BEETS

¾ cup sugar

¾ cup water

1 large onion, halved lengthwise, thinly sliced

¾ cup vinegar

1 teaspoon salt

2 cans sliced beets, not drained

Combine the sugar, vinegar, water, salt, and sliced onion. Bring to a boil and simmer for 5 minutes. Remove from the heat and stir in the beets. Let stand at room temperature for 1 hour. Refrigerate overnight before serving.

HOLIDAY SALAD

1 package orange gelatin mix

1 small can drained Mandarin oranges

¼ cup chopped pecans (optional)

1 cup boiling water

1 can jellied cranberry sauce

Mix the gelatin and the boiling water. Add the cranberry sauce and stir until smooth. Add the orange sections and the nuts. Refrigerate until firm before serving.

NOTE: This salad is pretty when gelled in a small mold.

MAMRINATED ARTICHOKES

2 cans artichoke hearts, drained

¼ cup canola or vegetable oil

½ teaspoon garlic salt

½ teaspoon onion powder

¼ cup lemon juice from bottle

¼ cup vinegar

1 teaspoon Italian seasoning

Put the artichokes into a container with a lid. Combine the remaining ingredients and mix with the artichokes. Chill overnight.

MARINATED VEGETABLE SALAD

¼ cup sugar

½ cup chopped onion

¾ cup cider vinegar

1 can peas, drained

1 can French cut green beans, drained

1 can sliced mushrooms, drained

1 can corn, drained

Combine the sugar and vinegar. Mix the onion and drained vegetables together. Pour the dressing over and mix well. Chill up to 8 hours before serving.

PEA AND PEANUT SALAD

2 cans peas, drained

6 pieces precooked bacon, chopped

½ cup mayonnaise

1 cup dry roasted peanuts

¼ cup chopped onion

¼ cup prepared Italian salad dressing

Combine the mayonnaise and the salad dressing. Mix the remaining ingredients and pour the dressing over. Mix well. Chill.

NOTE: 1 can of chopped water chestnuts may be substituted for the peanuts.

PEA SALAD

2 cans peas, drained

¼ cup canned ham cut into ¼" pieces

¼ cup mayonnaise

1 can sliced mushrooms, drained

¼ cup Cheddar cheese, diced

1 teaspoon prepared mustard

Mix the mayonnaise and mustard. Combine the remaining ingredients. Pour the mayonnaise over and mix well. Chill.

PICKLED ONIONS

1 cup water

¼ cup sugar or sweetener

2 medium onions sliced and separated into rings

1 cup vinegar

3 cinnamon sticks

½ teaspoon salt

Mix the water, vinegar, sugar, cinnamon sticks, and salt in a pan. Bring to a boil, cover and reduce the heat. Simmer for 10 minutes. Remove the cinnamon sticks and pour the hot mixture over the onion rings. Refrigerate at least overnight before serving.

PINEAPPLE SALAD

1 20 oz can pineapple chunks, drained

1 tablespoon lemon juice

¼ teaspoon vanilla flavoring

½ cup chopped pecans or walnuts

1/4 cup mayonnaise

Mix the mayonnaise, lemon juice, and vanilla. Stir into the pineapple and chopped nuts. Chill before serving.

SAUCES AND DRESSINGS

Basic Vinaigrette

Cocktail Sauce

Easy Mushroom Sauce

Eggless Mayonnaise

Lemon Garlic Grilling Sauce

Mock Hollandaise Sauce

Remoulade Sauce

Roasted Red Pepper Sauce

Spicy Mustard Sauce

Sweet Mustard Sauce

Tartar Sauce

Tomato Rarebit Sauce

Welch Rarebit Sauce

BASIC VINAIGRETTE

1/3 cup balsamic vinegar

1 ½ teaspoons garlic powder

Salt, pepper to taste

1 teaspoon dry mustard

¾ cup olive oil or canola oil

Mix the vinegar, mustard, and garlic powder. Stir in the olive oil in a stream, blending well. Season with the salt and pepper to taste.

NOTE: This makes a great marinate for seafood, chicken, and meats.
NOTE: ¼ teaspoon dried basil may be added.

COCKTAIL SAUCE

½ cup ketchup

1 tablespoon lemon or lime juice

2 drops hot sauce

1 tablespoon prepared mustard

½ teaspoon garlic powder

salt, pepper to taste

Mix well and chill before serving.

EASY MUSHROOM SAUCE

1 can cream of mushroom soup

1 teaspoon prepared mustard

½ cup Cheddar cheese

¾ cup milk made from dry

1 egg, beaten

1 tablespoon grated Parmesan cheese

Stir the milk, mustard, and soup in a small saucepan until blended. Cook for 2 to 3 minutes until heated. Beat the egg and temper the mixture by stirring a little of the soup mixture into the egg and blending well; then stir the egg into the sauce. Cook over low heat until the mixture thickens, stirring constantly. Do not boil the mixture. Remove from the heat and stir in the cheeses, stirring until they are melted. Serve warm over vegetables and chicken.

EGGLESS MAYONNAISE

1 teaspoon powdered sugar

¼ cup milk made from dry

¼ teaspoon dry mustard

2 tablespoons vinegar or lemon juice

1 cup vegetable or canola oil   ½ teaspoon salt
2 tablespoons evaporated milk

Chill the oil and milk. Put the sugar, salt, mustard, and milk made from the dry mix into a bowl. Beat well. Add ¼ cup of the oil and beat well. Alternately add the remaining oil and vinegar (or lemon juice). Beat well after each addition. Add the evaporated milk and beat well. This makes 1½ cups.

LEMON GARLIC GRILLING SAUCE

¼ cup melted butter   ¼ cup olive or canola oil
¼ cup lemon juice   1 tablespoon Worcestershire sauce
1 ½ teaspoons garlic powder

Combine all ingredients until well blended. Brush on fish, chicken, seafood, or vegetables when grilling.

MOCK HOLLANDAISE SAUCE

½ cup mayonnaise   1 tablespoon lemon juice
3 tablespoons water

Combine all ingredients in a saucepan. Stir with a wire whisk until smooth. Cook the mixture over low heat, stirring constantly for 3 to 4 minutes until heated. Serve warm.

NOTE: This sauce is also very good when 1 tablespoon of prepared mustard is added.

REMOULADE SAUCE

1 cup mayonnaise   1 ½ teaspoons garlic powder
2 tablespoons very finely chopped onion   1 tablespoon prepared mustard
1 teaspoon dry parsley flakes   ½ teaspoon Greek or Italian seasoning

Combine all ingredients. Chill. Serve with fish or seafood.

ROASTED RED PEPPER SAUCE

½ cup chopped onion

1 12 oz jar roasted red peppers, drained

1 cup water

½ cup cream, from canned

1 tablespoon butter

2 chicken bouillon cubes

1 teaspoon corn starch

½ cup Parmesan cheese

Sauté the onion in the butter for 2 minutes until tender. Stir in the corn starch. Finely chop the roasted red peppers. Mix the bouillon cubes and the water. Add the chopped peppers and the water. Cook over medium heat for 5 minutes until hot. Stir in the canned cream and the Parmesan cheese. Cook only until heated through, do not boil.

NOTE: This sauce is great over pasta and also over seafood cakes.

SPICY MUSTARD SAUCE

½ cup mayonnaise

¼ teaspoon hot sauce (optional)

3 tablespoons spicy mustard

Mix all ingredients and serve as a sauce for fish dishes.

SWEET MUSTARD SAUCE

2 tablespoons brown sugar

2 tablespoons flour

½ cup water

1 tablespoon vinegar

2 tablespoons butter

½ cup canned cream

¼ cup prepared mustard

¼ teaspoon ginger (optional)

Combine the brown sugar and butter in a small pan and cook over low heat until the sugar dissolves. Add the flour and stir until smooth. Cook for 1 minute, stirring constantly. Slowly add the canned cream which has been mixed with the water, stirring constantly. Cook until thickened. Stir in the mustard, vinegar, and ginger.

NOTE: ¾ cup of milk prepared from powdered milk mix may be substituted for the canned cream and the water.

TARTAR SAUCE

½ cup mayonnaise
2 teaspoons lemon or lime juice from bottle

2 tablespoons drained pickle relish

Mix well and chill before serving.

TOMATO RAREBIT SAUCE

1 can undiluted tomato soup
½ teaspoon garlic powder

1 teaspoon Worcestershire sauce
2 cup grated Cheddar cheese

Combine all ingredients and cook on medium heat until the cheese is melted.

NOTE: This sauce is good when served over salmon loaf, salmon or tuna cakes, chicken loaf.

WELSH RAREBIT SAUCE

2 tablespoons butter
3 tablespoons all purpose flour
1 12 oz can beer or milk made from dry
2 drops hot sauce

2 tablespoons vegetable or canola oil
1 tablespoon dry mustard
2 cups grated Cheddar cheese
salt, pepper to taste

Melt the butter and oil. Mix the flour and the dry mustard into the butter mixture. Cook for 1 minute. Add the liquid and whisk until smooth. Cook over medium heat 5 minutes until thickened. Stir in the cheese and seasonings and cook over very low heat for 5 to 10 minutes until the cheese is thickened.
Serve over toast for a main entrée.

NOTE: This sauce is equally good when served over salmon loaf, salmon or tuna cakes, chicken loaf, or when stirred into cooked macaroni.

SEAFOOD

CLAMS

Baked Clams

Clam Fritters

Clam Fritters another Way

Clam Pizza

Clam Sauce with Linguini

Red Clam Sauce with Spaghetti

Stuffed Clams

CRAB

Cheesy Crab and Rice

Crab and Fettuccini

Crab with Mushrooms

Lemon Crab with Pasta

OYSTERS

Green Bean and Oyster Casserole

Fried Oysters

Roasted Oysters

Scalloped Corn and Oysters

SALMON

Mini Salmon Loaves

Salmon and Vegetable Bake

Salmon Cakes

Salmon Cakes with Mustard Gravy

Salmon Casserole

Salmon Loaf

Salmon Pot Pie

Salmon Shepherd's Pie

Smoked Salmon Salad

TUNA

Fancy Tuna Salad

Mini Tuna Loaves

Seafood Salad

Shoestring Potato &Tuna Casserole

Tuna Alfredo

Tuna and Cheese Pasta

Tuna Nicoise

Tuna Patties

Tuna Pie

Tuna Salad

Tuna Spaghetti

CLAMS

BAKED CLAMS

¼ cup butter, melted

1 tablespoon Parmesan cheese

2 teaspoons lemon juice

1 ½ teaspoons garlic powder

½ teaspoon pepper

¾ cup commercial seasoned bread crumbs

1 teaspoon dried parsley

¼ teaspoon lemon zest if using real lemon

2 teaspoons dried chives

3 7 oz cans minced clams

Drain the minced clams and reserve the juice. Mix the clams and the remaining ingredients together, adding the reserved clam juice to just moisten the ingredients. Spoon the mixture into individual casserole dishes or into clam shells which have been coated with cooking spray. Bake at 350 for 20 to 25 minutes until lightly browned.

CLAM FRITTERS

1 ½ cups soft bread crumbs

2 eggs, separated

2 drops hot sauce

2 7 oz cans minced clams, well drained

1 teaspoon dried parsley leaves

½ teaspoon salt

Separate the eggs. Beat the egg whites until stiff. Beat the egg yolks. Mix the yolks, clams, and seasonings. Stir into egg whites. Form the mixture into small patties and fry in a skillet that has been lightly oiled.

CLAM FRITTERS ANOTHER WAY

2 7 oz cans minced clams, well drained

1 cup baking mix

½ teaspoon salt

1 teaspoon dried chives

1 egg, beaten

½ cup evaporated milk

½ teaspoon pepper

1 tablespoon finely chopped onion

Beat the egg and mix with the milk and spices. Stir into the baking mix. Add the drained clams. Fry in small mounds in a lightly greased skillet.

NOTE: These are good as an entrée or as an appetizer.

CLAM PIZZA

1 12" precooked pizza crust

1 can sliced mushrooms, drained

½ cup grated Cheddar cheese

1 4 oz can of sliced black olives, drained

1 package dry Alfredo sauce mix

1 7 to 8 oz can minced clams, drained

1 tablespoon grated Parmesan cheese

Mix the Alfredo sauce according to package directions. Use 6 to 8 tablespoons of the sauce to top the pizza crust. Top with the clams, mushrooms, and the olives. Mix the cheeses and sprinkle over the pizza. Bake at 350 for 15 minutes until bubbly.

CLAM SAUCE WITH LINGUINI

1 7 to 8 oz can minced clams, drained

2 teaspoons dried parsley flakes

2/3 cup clam juice or chicken broth

2 to 3 cups of hot cooked linguini

½ teaspoon garlic powder

½ teaspoon pepper

1/3 cup chopped walnuts

1/3 cup grated Parmesan cheese

Mix the clams, juice, and spices. Cook over medium heat until near boiling. Toast the chopped walnuts. Top the linguini with the clam mixture, sprinkle with the nuts and the cheese.

RED CLAM SAUCE FOR SPAGHETTI

½ cup chopped onion

1 teaspoon garlic powder

2 8 oz cans minced clams, not drained

1 12 oz can tomato paste

Salt, pepper to taste

Grated Parmesan cheese

1 tablespoon oil

1 teaspoon dried basil, crushed

1 can diced tomatoes

1 4 oz can sliced mushrooms, drained

Cooked spaghetti

Sauté the onion in the oil for 2 minutes until tender. Mix the spices, clams, tomatoes, tomato paste, and mushrooms. Put into a slow cooker. Cook on low heat for 4 to 6 hours. Serve over the spaghetti.. Top with grated Parmesan cheese.

STUFFED CLAMS

¼ cup chopped onion
1 7 oz can minced clams, drained
Water and reserved clam juice

1 tablespoons butter
1 cup chicken flavored stuffing mix

Sauté the onion in the butter for 2 minutes until tender. Stir in the drained clams. Stir the reserved clam juice into the stuffing mix and stir. If necessary, add water, 1 teaspoon at a time until the stuffing mix is moistened. Stir into clams and mound into 2 scallop shells that have been coated with cooking spray. Bake at 350 for 20 minutes until lightly browned.

CRAB

CHEESY CRAB AND RICE

2 7 oz cans crab, drained
1 cup processed cheese food, grated
1 4 oz can sliced mushrooms, drained
Hot cooked rice

1 can cream of chicken soup
1 teaspoon dried chives
½ cup canned mixed vegetables, drained

Combine the crab, soup, cheese, chives, mushrooms, and vegetables. Heat to boiling and reduce the heat. Simmer for 5 minutes and serve over the rice.

CRAB FETTUCCINI

8 oz fettuccini or spaghetti
4 tablespoons canola oil
1 tablespoon dried parsley flakes
½ cup dry white wine (or chicken broth)
2 7 oz cans crab meat, drained

1 teaspoon dried basil, crushed
1 teaspoon garlic powder
1 teaspoon dried chives
2 teaspoons soy sauce
Grated Parmesan cheese

Cook the noodles as directed, drain, and keep warm. Mix the spices, wine, and crab meat. Simmer until bubbly. Pour over the noodles and top each serving with the Parmesan cheese.

CRAB WITH MUSHROOMS

2 7 oz cans crab, drained
1 8 oz can tomato sauce
¼ teaspoon onion powder
½ teaspoon pepper
Hot cooked rice

1 4 oz can sliced mushrooms, drained
¼ teaspoon garlic powder
1 teaspoon dried chives
¼ cup water

Mix the crab, mushrooms, sauce, water, and spices. Bring to a boil and reduce the heat. Simmer for 5 minutes. Serve over the rice.

LEMON CRAB WITH PASTA

8 oz corkscrew pasta
½ cup butter
1 teaspoon dried chives
½ teaspoon garlic powder

1 chicken bouillon cube
2 tablespoons lemon juice
½ teaspoon dried parsley
2 7 oz cans crab, drained

Cook the pasta in boiling water with the bouillon cube as directed on the package. Drain the pasta. Melt the butter and stir in the remaining ingredients. Pour over the pasta and mix. If desired, grated Parmesan cheese may be added to each serving.

OYSTERS

FRIED OYSTERS

2 7 oz cans whole oysters
½ teaspoon pepper
2 eggs
Oil for frying

1 cup saltine cracker crumbs
½ cup all purpose flour
2 tablespoons water

Drain the oysters and pat them dry with a paper towel. Beat the eggs and water. Mix the crumbs and pepper and put in a mound on waxed paper. Put the flour in a mound on waxed paper. Coat the oysters first in the flour, then in the egg, then in the cracker crumbs. Put on waxed paper and allow the coating to dry for 15 minutes. Heat 1" of oil in a skillet and gently put the oysters into the oil. Cook, turning once, until both sides are golden browned.

GREEN BEAN AND OYSTER CASSEROLE

1 can cut green beans, drained	1 can cream of celery soup
½ cup water	¼ teaspoon salt
½ teaspoon pepper	¼ teaspoon Worcestershire sauce
1 cup canned oysters	½ cup of the oyster liquid
½ cup butter, melted	2 cups saltine cracker crumbs

Combine the cracker crumbs, melted butter, salt, and pepper. Place 1/3 of the cracker crumbs into a baking dish that has been coated with cooking spray. Drain the oysters and reserve ½ cup of the liquid. Dice the oysters. Cover the crumbs with half of the green beans and half of the oysters. Repeat the layers. Heat the soup, water, oyster liquid, and the Worcestershire sauce. Pour the soup mixture over the oysters and top with the remaining 1/3 of the cracker crumbs. Bake at 350 for 40 minutes until bubbly.

ROASTED OYSTERS

2 7 oz cans whole oysters	1 can spinach
1 cup round buttery cracker crumbs	¼ cup butter

Drain the oysters and put in a single layer in a baking dish that has been coated with cooking spray. Drain the spinach and squeegee dry. Put 1 teaspoon of the spinach over each oyster. Melt the butter and mix with the crumbs. Sprinkle the mixture over the oysters. Bake at 350 for 20 minutes until the crumb topping begins to brown.

SCALLOPED CORN AND OYSTERS

1 can cream style corn	1 cup saltine cracker crumbs
1 cup evaporated milk	1 egg, beaten
¼ teaspoon salt	½ teaspoon pepper
1 cup canned oysters, drained	½ cup buttery round cracker crumbs
2 tablespoons butter, melted	

Combine the corn, saltines, milk, egg, salt, and pepper. Dice the oysters and stir into the mixture. Pour into a baking dish that has been coated with cooking spray. Mix the melted butter and the buttery cracker crumbs and sprinkle on top. Bake at 350 for 30 minutes until bubbly.

SALMON

MINI SALMON LOAVES

¼ cup chopped onion
1 16 oz can salmon
¼ cup finely chopped onions

1 tablespoons butter
2 cups chicken flavored stuffing mix
1 tablespoon dried chives

Sauté the onion in the butter for 2 minutes until tender. Drain the salmon and remove the skin and bones. Prepare the stuffing mix as directed on the package. Mix all ingredients and put the mixture into 6 muffin cups which have been liberally coated with cooking spray. Bake at 350 for 20 minutes until lightly browned.

SALMON AND VEGETABLE BAKE

1 16 oz can salmon
½ cup grated Cheddar cheese
1½ cups milk made from dry
1 teaspoon paprika
½ teaspoon pepper

1 can mixed vegetables, drained
½ cup baking mix
2 teaspoons spicy mustard
½ teaspoon dried parsley flakes
2 eggs, beaten

Drain the salmon and remove the skin and bones. Mix the salmon and the vegetables. Beat the remaining ingredients together and combine with the salmon. Pour into a baking dish that has been coated with cooking spray. Bake at 350 for 45 minutes.

SALMON CAKES

1 16 oz can salmon
8 saltine crackers
¼ cup grated Cheddar cheese

1 beaten egg
¼ cup finely chopped onion
1 teaspoon dried chives

Drain the salmon and remove the skin and bones. Mix all ingredients well and form into 1 ¼" balls. Flatten the balls. Fry the salmon cakes in a skillet which has been coated with cooking spray. Spray the tops of the salmon cakes with cooking spray before turning them.

SALMON CAKES WITH MUSTARD GRAVY

1 16 oz can salmon
8 saltine crackers
¼ cup grated Cheddar cheese
½ teaspoon chicken bouillon granules
1 tablespoons butter
1 cup chicken broth or water
1 tablespoon flour

1 beaten egg
¼ cup finely chopped onion
1 teaspoon dried parsley
½ teaspoon pepper
2 teaspoons prepared spicy mustard
1 teaspoon dried chives

Drain the salmon and remove the skin and bones. Mix the salmon, egg, crackers, cheese, and chives well. Form into 4 patties. Fry the salmon cakes in a skillet which has been coated with cooking spray. Spray the tops of the salmon cakes with cooking spray before turning them.

Melt the butter. Stir in the flour and whisk until smooth; slowly add the broth and spices. Whisk until smooth and cook on medium heat for 4 to 5 minutes until the mixture begins to thicken. Serve the mustard sauce over the salmon cakes.

SALMON CASSEROLE

2 cans sliced potatoes, drained
1 can cream of chicken soup
¼ cup chopped onion
2 drops hot sauce
2 tablespoons melted butter
½ cup round buttery cracker crumbs

2 7 oz pouches salmon
½ cup canned peas, drained
2 teaspoons prepared mustard
1 teaspoon dried chives
2 tablespoons grated Cheddar cheese

Stir the soup, onion, mustard, hot sauce, and chives together. Stir the soup mixture into the potatoes, salmon, and the peas. Pour into a baking dish that has been coated with cooking spray and bake at 350 for 25 minutes.

Melt the butter and cool. Stir the cheese and cracker crumbs into the butter. Sprinkle over the casserole and bake an additional 5 minutes until the crumbs are lightly browned.

NOTE: A 16 oz can of salmon may be substituted for the salmon pouches. Remove the skin and bones.

SALMON LOAF

1 16 oz can salmon, drained
1 ½ cups saltine cracker crumbs
1 egg, beaten
½ cup grated Cheddar cheese

1 egg
2 teaspoons lemon juice
¼ cup finely chopped onion
1 teaspoon dried chives

Remove the skin and the bones from the salmon. Mix all ingredients well and shape into a small loaf. Put into a baking dish that has been coated with cooking spray. Bake at 350 for 45 minutes until lightly browned. Let the loaf set for 10 minutes before slicing.

SALMON POT PIE

1 cup self rising flour
1 cup milk made from dry
1 cup canned cut baby corn, drained
1 cup green beans, drained

½ cup melted butter
1 16 oz can salmon, drained
1 can whole potatoes, drained
1 can cream of chicken soup

Mix the flour, melted butter, and milk. Remove the skin and the bones from the salmon. Dice the potatoes. Mix the potatoes, salmon, corn, beans, and soup. Pour into a pie plate that has been coated with cooking spray. Pour the flour batter over the salmon mixture. Put the pie plate on a baking tray that has been lined with aluminum foil to catch any drips as the pie bakes. Bake at 350 for 35 to 45 minutes until the top crust is lightly browned.

NOTE: 2 cans of mixed vegetables, drained, may be substituted for baby corn, green beans, and potatoes.

SALMON SHEPHERD'S PIE

1 package instant mashed potato flakes
2 cans mixed vegetables, drained
½ cup grated Cheddar cheese

1 16 oz can salmon, drained
1 can cream of chicken soup

Make the mashed potatoes as directed on the package. Remove the skin and bones from the salmon. Combine the salmon, vegetables, and soup. Pour into an 8" baking dish that has been coated with cooking spray. Top with the mashed potatoes. Bake at 350 for 30 minutes. Top with the cheese and bake an additional 5 minutes.

SMOKED SALMON SALAD

1 16 oz can salmon, drained	¼ cup finely chopped onion
1/3 cup mayonnaise	¼ cup pickle relish
½ to 1 teaspoon hickory smoke flavoring	2 teaspoons lemon juice

Remove the skin and bones from the salmon. Mix all ingredients and chill before serving.

NOTE: This makes a good sandwich spread. Try it as a spread with crackers for an appetizer.

TUNA

FANCY TUNA SALAD

1 7 oz can tuna, drained	2 tablespoons finely chopped onion
¼ cup chopped walnuts	¼ cup grated Cheddar cheese
¼ cup mayonnaise	2 teaspoons lemon juice

Mix all ingredients and chill before serving. This is good as a sandwich filling or mounded on a small plate for a light lunch.

MINI TUNA LOAVES

¼ cup chopped onion	1 tablespoons butter
2 7 oz cans tuna, drained	2 cups chicken flavored stuffing mix
¼ cup grated Cheddar cheese	1 tablespoon dried chives

Sauté the onion in the butter for 2 minutes until tender. Prepare the stuffing mix as directed on the package. Mix all ingredients and put the mixture into 6 muffin cups which have been liberally coated with cooking spray. Bake at 350 for 20 minutes until lightly browned.

SEAFOOD SALAD

1 7 oz can tuna, drained	1 7 oz can shrimp, drained
2 teaspoons lemon juice	2 hard boiled eggs, diced
2 tablespoons finely chopped onion	½ cup mayonnaise
Salt, pepper to taste	

Sprinkle the shrimp and the tuna with lemon juice and mix. Stir all ingredients together and chill. This makes a good sandwich filling or is good as a light lunch when mounded onto small plates and served with crackers.

SHOESTRING POTATO AND TUNA CASSEROLE

1 4 oz can shoestring potatoes

1 7 oz can tuna, drained

1 4 oz can sliced mushrooms, drained

1 can cream of chicken soup

1 6 oz can evaporated milk

Reserve 1 cup of the potatoes as a topping. Mix the remaining potatoes with the other ingredients. Pour into a baking dish which has been coated with cooking spray. Bake at 350 for 30 minutes until bubbly. Coarsely crush the reserved potatoes and sprinkle over the casserole. Bake an additional 5 minutes.

NOTE: Canned peas and/or carrots may be added to this casserole.

TUNA ALFREDO

8 oz spaghetti or linguini

1 can peas, drained

½ cup milk made from dry

2 7 oz cans tuna, drained

½ teaspoon pepper

1 chicken bouillon cube

1 can cream of mushroom soup

½ cup grated Parmesan cheese

1 can sliced mushrooms, drained

Cook the pasta in boiling water with the bouillon cube. Drain and keep warm. Mix the remaining ingredients and cook over medium heat for 10 minutes. Add the pasta and cook 5 more minutes.

TUNA AND CHEESE PASTA

2 ½ cups cooked pasta

¼ cup milk made from dry

1 teaspoon chicken bouillon granules

1 7 oz can tuna, drained

8 oz processed cheese food

1 tablespoon ketchup

1 prepared mustard

½ cup canned peas, drained

Combine the milk and cheese with the bouillon, ketchup, and mustard. Cook on medium heat until the cheese has melted and the mixture is bubbly. Stir in the pasta, peas, and tuna and mix well. Cook 5 more minutes, stirring frequently.

TUNA CASSEROLE

8 oz noodles
½ cup finely diced onion
1 can cream of chicken soup
Salt, pepper to taste

1 chicken bouillon cube
1 tablespoon butter
2 7 oz cans tuna, drained

Cook the noodles in boiling water with the chicken bouillon cube. Sauté the onion in butter for 2 minutes until tender. Stir the soup, tuna, and onion together. Stir into the noodles. Salt and pepper to taste. Bake at 350 for 30 minutes.

NOTE: Grated cheese, crushed potato chips, or French fried onion rings may be put over the baked casserole. Bake 5 additional minutes.

TUNA NICOISE

1 can whole potatoes, drained
2 7 oz cans tuna, drained
1 4 oz can sliced black olives, drained
1 tablespoon prepared spicy mustard

1 can whole green beans, drained
2 hard boiled eggs, peeled
2 tablespoons red wine vinegar
3 tablespoons oil

Quarter the whole potatoes and the boiled eggs. Mix the vinegar, mustard, and oil together. Arrange the potatoes, green beans, eggs, olives, and tuna on 2 plates. Pour the dressing over.

TUNA PATTIES

1 7 oz can tuna
¼ teaspoon salt
1 teaspoon dried chives

¼ cup saltine cracker crumbs
1 beaten egg

Drain the tuna. Mix all ingredients well and shape into 3 patties. Fry in a lightly greased skillet until both sides are golden brown.

TUNA PIE

1 unbaked pie crust	2 7 oz cans tuna, drained
1 cup grated Cheddar cheese	¼ cup finely chopped onion
3 eggs, beaten	1 cup mayonnaise
½ cup evaporated milk	1 teaspoon dried chives

Pierce the pie crust with a fork and bake at 375 for 10 minutes. Mix the tuna, cheese, and onions and put into the pie crust. Stir the eggs, mayonnaise, milk, and chives together and pour over the tuna mixture. Do not mix. Bake at 375 for 45 to 50 minutes.

TUNA SALAD

2 7 oz cans tuna, drained	¼ cup finely chopped onion
1/3 cup mayonnaise	¼ cup pickle relish

Mix all ingredients and chill before serving.

NOTE: This makes a good sandwich spread. It can also be served mounded on a small plate for a light lunch. Try it as a spread with crackers for an appetizer.

TUNA SPAGHETTI

3 cups cooked spaghetti	1 chicken bouillon cube
1 cup grated Cheddar cheese	1 7 oz can tuna, drained
1 14 oz jar spaghetti sauce	½ teaspoon garlic powder
½ teaspoon onion powder	½ teaspoon pepper
1 tablespoon grated Parmesan cheese	

Cook the pasta in boiling water with the bouillon cube. Mix the spaghetti sauce with the spices. Mix in the tuna cheese, and the pasta. Sprinkle with the Parmesan cheese. Bake at 350 for 25 to 30 minutes until bubbly.

SIDE DISHES

Apples and Pineapple

Apricot Glazed Carrots

Asparagus Casserole

Baked Beans

Baked Pineapple

Carrot Casserole

Cheesy Green Beans

Cheesy Mashed Potatoes

Corn Pudding

Fancy Peas

Fried Potatoes

Fruited Carrots

Fruited Rice

German Potato Salad

Green Bean and Potato Casserole

Green Beans with Walnuts

Hawaiian Baked Beans

Jalapeno and Corn Casserole

Lima Bean Casserole

Mashed Sweet Potatoes

Mexican Corn

Mexican Rice

Mixed Beans

Mixed Vegetable Casserole

Navy and Pinto Beans

Pineapple Beets

Potato Cakes

Potato Salad

Potatoes and Parsley

Potatoes and Peas

Potatoes in Cheesy Mustard Sauce

Potatoes with Lemon and Chives

Rice Casserole

Scalloped Potatoes

Slow Cooker Beans & Potatoes

Stuffed Beans

Stuffed Onions

Sweet Potato Balls

Sweet Potato Casserole

Sweet Potatoes and Fruit

Sweet Potatoes and Garlic Sauce

Vegetable Casserole

Vegetable Medley

APPLES AND PINEAPPLE

2 cans fried apples, drained
½ teaspoon ground cinnamon

1 8 oz can pineapple tidbits, not drained

Combine all ingredients and cook on low heat for 10 minutes until heated.

APRICOT GLAZED CARROTS

1 can whole carrots, drained
¼ cup apricot jam

1 tablespoon butter

Combine the butter and the jam and cook on low heat until the jam is dissolved. Stir in the carrots and heat.

ASPARAGUS CASSEROLE

2 cans asparagus, drained
½ cup grated Cheddar cheese
2 tablespoons melted butter

1 4 oz can sliced mushrooms, drained
½ cup buttery cracker crumbs

Put the asparagus spears into a baking dish. Top with the mushrooms, then the cheese. Mix the cracker crumbs with the melted butter and sprinkle over the top. Bake at 350 for 15 to 20 minutes.

BAKED BEANS

2 cans pork and beans
¼ cup prepared BBQ sauce
2 teaspoons prepared spicy mustard

¼ cup finely chopped onion
1 tablespoon brown sugar
1 teaspoon garlic powder

Drain the cans of beans in a colander for at least 15 minutes. Mix all ingredients and pour into a baking dish that has been coated with cooking spray. Bake at 350 for 20 minutes until bubbly.

BAKED PINEAPPLE

1 20 oz can pineapple tidbits
1 cup grated Cheddar cheese
½ cup butter

½ cup sugar
3 tablespoons all purpose flour
3/4 cup round buttery crackers, crumbled

Drain the pineapple and reserve 3 tablespoons of the juice. Mix the juice, flour, and sugar together and stir into the pineapple. Pour into a 1 quart baking dish that has been coated with cooking spray. Melt the butter and stir into the cracker crumbs. Sprinkle the crumbs evenly over the pineapple and bake at 350 for 25 minutes.

CARROT CASSEROLE

2 cans crinkle cut carrots, drained
1 can sliced water chestnuts, drained
¼ cup grated Cheddar cheese
1 cup round buttery cracker crumbs

1 can peas, drained
1 can cream of chicken soup
¼ cup melted butter

Combine the carrots, peas, chestnuts, soup, and cheese. Pour into a baking dish that has been coated with cooking spray Combine the crumbs and the butter and sprinkle over the top of the casserole. Bake at 350 for 30 minutes.

CHEESY GREEN BEANS

2 cans French sliced green beans, drained
1 can cream of chicken soup
½ teaspoon garlic powder
1 8 oz can sliced water chestnuts, drained
½ cup sliced almonds

¼ cup milk made from dry
1 teaspoon dehydrated onion flakes
½ teaspoon pepper
1 cup grated Cheddar cheese

Coarsely chop the water chestnuts. Stir the milk, soup, and spices together and add the water chestnuts, beans, and cheese. Pour into a baking dish that has been coated with cooking spray. Bake at 350 for 40 minutes. Top with the almonds and bake an additional 5 minutes.

CHEESY MASHED POTATOES

1 package instant mashed potato flakes
1 tablespoon canned bacon bits

½ cup grated Cheddar cheese

Prepare the mashed potatoes as directed on the package. Stir the cheese into the hot potatoes until melted. Garnish the potatoes with the bacon bits.

CORN PUDDING

2 tablespoons butter
1 1/3 cups milk made from dry
2 eggs, well beaten

2 tablespoons all purpose flour
salt, pepper to taste
2 cans corn, drained

Melt the butter and whisk in the flour. Gradually add the milk, whisking until smooth. Bring to the boiling point. Add the corn, salt, and pepper. Remove from the heat and whisk in the eggs. Pour into a baking dish that has been coated with cooking spray. Bake at 350 for 30 minutes.

FANCY PEAS

¼ cup chopped onion
1 4 oz can sliced mushrooms, drained
1 can peas, drained

2 tablespoons butter
2 tablespoons chopped walnuts
salt, pepper to taste

Sauté the onion in butter for 2 minutes until soft. Add the mushrooms and the walnuts and sauté for 2 more minutes. Stir in the peas, salt, and pepper.

FRIED POTATOES

2 cans whole potatoes, drained
½ teaspoon salt
¼ teaspoon garlic powder
2 tablespoons Parmesan cheese

2 tablespoons oil
½ teaspoon pepper
¼ teaspoon paprika

Dice the potatoes and mix with the salt, pepper, garlic, and paprika. Put the oil in a skillet. Put the potatoes into the skillet and fry on medium heat for 15 minutes until the potatoes are slightly browned. Sprinkle with the Parmesan cheese before serving.

FRUITED CARROTS

1 can crinkle cut carrots, sliced
¼ cup boiling water
½ teaspoon lemon juice

¼ cup dried cranberries
1 tablespoon butter

Put the cranberries into the boiling water. Turn off the heat and let them soak for 10 minutes until tender.
Stir in the remaining ingredients and heat.

FRUITED RICE

¼ cup chopped onion
2 ½ cups water
1 cup raw rice
¼ cup pecans, chopped

1 tablespoon butter
1 chicken bouillon cube
½ cup dried cranberries

Sauté the onion in the butter for 2 minutes until tender. Add the rice and sauté for 3 more minutes. Add the remaining ingredients and bring to a boil. Reduce the heat and simmer for 15 to 20 minutes until the water is absorbed.

GERMAN POTATO SALAD

2 cans sliced potatoes, drained
2 tablespoons canola or vegetable oil
1 tablespoon pickle relish
½ cup vinegar
½ teaspoon pepper

2 tablespoons bacon bits
½ cup chopped onion
¼ cup water
½ teaspoon salt
1 tablespoon prepared spicy mustard

Sauté the onion in the oil for 2 minutes until tender. Add the water, vinegar, salt, pepper, and mustard and heat to the boiling point. Stir in the sliced potatoes and the bacon bits. Serve warm or room temperature.

GREEN BEAN AND POTATO CASSEROLE

½ cup chopped onion

1 can cut green beans, drained

1 4 oz can sliced mushrooms, drained

½ cup water

1 cup grated Cheddar cheese

2 tablespoons butter

1 can sliced potatoes, drained

1 can cream of chicken soup

1 chicken bouillon cube

Sauté the onion in butter for 2 minutes until tender. Dice the potatoes. Mix the water and the bouillon cube. Stir in the soup and the onion. Mix in the remaining ingredients. Bake at 350 for 30 minutes until bubbly.

GREEN BEANS WITH WALNUTS

2 cans French sliced green beans

2 tablespoons butter

2 tablespoons soy sauce

¼ cup chopped walnuts

Drain the beans, reserving ¼ cup of the liquid. Mix the liquid with the other ingredients and cook on medium heat for 15 minutes, stirring frequently.

HAWAIIAN BAKED BEANS

1 28 oz can pork and beans

2 tablespoons prepared mustard

2 tablespoons brown sugar

1 8 oz can pineapple tidbits

2 tablespoons ketchup or BBQ sauce

Drain the beans and the pineapple well. Mix the mustard, sugar, and ketchup and stir into the beans. Pour into a baking dish which has been coated with cooking spray. Bake at 350 for 30 minutes.

JALAPENO AND CORN CASSEROLE

1 cup raw rice

½ cup butter

1 can cream style corn

½ cup grated Cheddar cheese

½ cup chopped onion

1 to 2 canned jalapeno peppers, minced

1 can yellow corn, drained

Cook the rice as directed on the package. Sauté the onion in the butter. Stir in the cooked rice, peppers, and corn. Pour into a baking dish that has been coated with cooking spray. Bake at 350 for 25 minutes. Top with the cheese and bake an additional 5 minutes.

LIMA BEAN CASSEROLE

2 cans lima beans, drained
1 cup round buttery cracker crumbs

3 slices precooked bacon
2 tablespoons butter, melted

Crumble the bacon and mix with the lima beans. Pour into a baking dish that has been coated with cooking spray. Mix the cracker crumbs and the butter and sprinkle over the lima beans. Bake at 350 for 20 minutes.

MASHED SWEET POTATOES

2 16 oz cans sweet potatoes, drained
1 tablespoon butter, melted

1 8 oz can crushed pineapple, drained
1 teaspoon ground cinnamon

Mix the sweet potatoes, cinnamon, and butter. Mash well. Stir in the crushed pineapple and pour the mixture into a baking dish that has been coated with cooking spray. Bake at 350 for 25 minutes.

MEXICAN CORN

1 can corn, drained
1/3 cup water
¼ teaspoon paprika

1 2 oz jar diced pimentos, drained
½ teaspoon pepper
½ teaspoon chili powder

Combine all ingredients and bring to a boil. Reduce the heat and cook for 5 minutes.

MEXICAN RICE

1 cup raw rice
¼ cup salsa
1 6 oz can tomato sauce
2 tablespoons oil

2 cups water
1 cup canned corn, drained
salt, pepper to taste

Lightly brown the rice in the oil on medium heat. Add the water and the tomato sauce and bring to a boil. Reduce the heat and add the salt, pepper, salsa, and corn. Cook, over low heat for 15 to 20 minutes until the liquid is absorbed.

MIXED BEANS

1 can navy beans, not drained

1 can pinto beans, rinsed and drained

1 tablespoon prepared spicy mustard

1 teaspoon onion powder

1 can kidney beans, rinsed and drained

½ cup diced country ham

½ teaspoon garlic powder

1 teaspoon dried pepper flakes

Combine all ingredients and bring to a boil. Reduce the heat and simmer for 10 minutes.

MIXED VEGETABLE CASSEROLE

1 can mixed vegetables, drained

1 can red beans, rinsed and drained

¼ cup chopped onion

1 cup round butter cracker crumbs

1 can lima beans, drained

1 cup cream of chicken soup

½ cup grated Cheddar cheese

¼ cup butter, melted

Combine the vegetables, onion, soup, and cheese. Pour into a baking dish that has been coated with cooking spray. Mix the cracker crumbs and the butter and sprinkle over the casserole. Bake at 350 for 30 minutes.

NAVY AND PINTO BEANS

1 can navy beans, not drained

½ cup diced country ham

1 can pinto beans, rinsed and drained

1 teaspoon dried pepper flakes

Mix all ingredients and bring to a boil. Reduce the heat and simmer for 10 minutes.

PINEAPPLE BEETS

1 8 oz can pineapple tidbits

¼ cup beet juice from canned beets

2 tablespoons brown sugar

1/8 teaspoon ground ginger

1 can sliced beets

2 ½ tablespoons white vinegar

1 ½ teaspoons corn starch

Drain the juice from the pineapple and mix with the beet juice. Stir in the vinegar, sugar, ginger, and corn starch. Cook over medium heat until it begins to thicken, stirring constantly. Add the beets and heat just to boiling. Just before serving, stir the pineapple in. Serve hot or warm.

POTATO CAKES

2 cups prepared instant mashed potatoes
¼ cup milk made from dry
1 beaten egg
¼ teaspoon onion powder

¼ cup baking mix
½ teaspoon vinegar
¼ teaspoon garlic powder
1 teaspoon dried parsley flakes

Mix the milk and the vinegar. Combine all ingredients. Form into 3" flattened patties and fry in skillet lightly coated with oil. Fry until golden brown on both sides.

POTATO SALAD

¾ cup mayonnaise
½ to 1 teaspoon salt
3 cans whole potatoes, drained
½ cup finely chopped onion

1 tablespoon prepared spicy mustard
¼ teaspoon pepper
2 chopped hard boiled eggs
½ cup pickle relish

Cube the canned potatoes. Mix the remaining ingredients and stir into the potatoes.

POTATOES AND PARSLEY

2 cans whole potatoes, drained
2 teaspoons dried parsley flakes

2 tablespoons butter
¼ cup water

Cut the potatoes in half. Melt the butter and stir in the potatoes and the parsley. Stir in the water and cook over medium until heated.

POTATOES AND PEAS

1 can whole potatoes, drained
1 can cream of celery soup

2 cans peas, drained
1/3 cup milk made from dry

Cut each canned potato into quarters. Mix the soup and the milk. Stir the potatoes and the peas into the soup mixture. Cook this on low heat for 10 to 15 minutes until heated through, stirring frequently.

POTATOES IN CHEESY MUSTARD SAUCE

2 cans whole potatoes, drained
½ cup milk made from dry
1 tablespoon butter

2 teaspoons prepared spicy mustard
1 tablespoon flour
½ cup grated Cheddar cheese

Combine the flour and butter and whisk until smooth. Cook over medium heat for 2 minutes. Stir in the milk and mustard and whisk until smooth. Stir in the cheese and cook until the mixture begins to thicken. Cut the potatoes in half and stir into the cheese sauce. Cook over low heat until heated.

POTATOES WITH LEMON AND CHIVES

2 cans whole potatoes, drained
2 teaspoons lemon juice from bottle
1 teaspoon dried chives
½ teaspoon pepper

¼ cup water
1 tablespoon butter
½ teaspoon chicken bouillon granules

Melt the butter and stir in the water, juice, and spices. Cut the potatoes in half and add to the butter mixture. Cook, over medium heat, stirring frequently, for 10 minutes.

RICE CASSEROLE

2 tablespoons slivered almonds
1/3 cup uncooked long grain rice
1 cup water
1 teaspoon lemon juice
1 4 oz can sliced mushrooms, drained

2 tablespoons chopped onion
3 tablespoons butter
1 chicken bouillon cube
½ teaspoon salt

Cook the almonds, onion, rice, and butter together for 5 minutes over high heat, stirring frequently. Mix the water, bouillon, lemon juice, and salt. Bring to a boil and cover. Reduce the heat and simmer for 15 minutes, stirring every 5 minutes. Add the mushrooms, cover, and cook 5 more minutes until the water is absorbed. Pour into a baking dish that has been coated with cooking spray. Bake at 350 for 20 to 25 minutes until it begins to brown lightly.

SCALLOPED POTATOES

½ cup chopped onion
2 cans sliced potatoes, well drained
1/3 cup milk made from dry
¼ teaspoon pepper

2 tablespoons butter
1 can cream of chicken soup
½ teaspoon salt

Sauté the onion in the butter for 2 minutes until tender. Gently mix all ingredients and pour into a baking dish which has been coated with cooking spray. Bake at 350 for 20 to 25 minutes until bubbly.

SLOW COOKER GREEN BEANS AND POTATOES

2 cans cut green beans
1 teaspoon chicken bouillon granules

1 can whole potatoes, drained
½ teaspoon pepper

Drain the green beans, reserving ½ cup of the juice. Mix the bouillon with the reserved juice and the pepper. Put the green beans into the slow cooker. Top with the potatoes. Pour the juice mixture over and cook on low for 4 to 6 hours or on high for 2 to 3 hours.

STUFFED BEANS

2 cans refried beans
½ teaspoon pepper
Cornmeal

1 teaspoon chili powder
¾" Cheddar cheese cubes
Oil for frying

Combine the beans, chili powder, and pepper. Wrap a small amount of the bean mixture around each cheese cube, pressing into a tight ball. Roll the beans in the cornmeal and gently drop into oil that has been heated to 350. Gently roll the balls in the oil and cook until they are browned.

STUFFED ONIONS

4 medium onions, approximately 2 ½" size
½ cup dry chicken flavored stuffing mix
1 can sliced water chestnuts, drained
½ cup water

2 slices precooked bacon, chopped
1 teaspoon dried parsley flakes
Salt, pepper to taste
1 beef bouillon cube

Peel the onions, leaving them whole. Put the onions into a pan of boiling water and cook for 6 minutes until tender. Let cool slightly, then scoop out 1 tablespoon from the top of each onion. Prepare the stuffing mix as directed on the package. Mix in the spices. Chop the water chestnuts and stir into the stuffing mixture. Divide the stuffing evenly among the onions. Bake uncovered at 350 for 30 to 40 minutes until tender. Mix the water and the bouillon cube. Baste the onions every 15 minutes with this mixture.

SWEET POTATO BALLS

2 cups of mashed sweet potatoes, from canned potatoes
¾ cup round buttery cracker crumbs
¼ cup butter
½ teaspoon vanilla

12 large size marshmallows
½ cup brown sugar
2 tablespoons water

Divide the mashed sweet potatoes into 12 portions. Mold each portion around a marshmallow and roll in the cracker crumbs. Mix the water, butter, and sugar and bring to a rolling boil. Stir in the vanilla. Put the sweet potato balls into a baking dish that has been coated with cooking spray. Pour the butter mixture over and bake at 350 for 15 minutes.

SWEET POTATO CASSEROLE

3 cups canned sweet potatoes, mashed
½ cup brown sugar
3 tablespoons butter, melted

1 egg, beaten
¼ cup all purpose flour
½ cup chopped nuts

Mash the sweet potatoes and mix in the beaten egg. Pour into a baking dish that has been coated with cooking spray. Mix the sugar, flour, butter, and nuts together and sprinkle evenly over the sweet potatoes. Bake at 350 for 30 minutes.

SWEET POTATOES AND FRUIT

2 16 oz cans sweet potatoes

1 8 oz can pineapple tidbits, drained

1 16 oz can fried apples, drained

1 teaspoon cinnamon

Mix all ingredients and cook over medium heat for 10 minutes.

SWEET POTATOES WITH GARLIC SAUCE

1 16 oz can sweet potatoes, drained

1/3 cup mayonnaise

¼ teaspoon pepper

½ teaspoon garlic powder

1 ½ tablespoons canola or vegetable oil

2 tablespoons water

Drain the sweet potatoes and put into a baking dish that has been coated with cooking spray. Bake at 350 for 20 minutes. Combine the mayonnaise, garlic, pepper, and water. Whisk in the oil and spread the mixture over the hot sweet potatoes.

VEGETABLE CASSEROLE

2 cans mixed vegetables, drained

½ cup grated processed cheese food

1 cup round buttery crackers, crushed

1/2 cup butter, divided

1 can cream of chicken soup

Drain the vegetables and put into a baking dish that has been coated with cooking spray. Melt ¼ cup butter and the cheese. Stir in the soup. Pour the mixture over the vegetables. Melt ¼ cup butter and mix with the cracker crumbs. Sprinkle over the soup mixture. Bake at 350 for 25 to 30 minutes.

VEGETABLE MEDLEY

1 can peas, drained

1 can green beans, drained

½ cup grated processed cheese food

1 can corn, drained

½ cup mayonnaise

Combine the corn, beans, and peas with the mayonnaise. Pour into a baking dish that has been coated with cooking spray. Top with the cheese and bake at 350 for 25 to 30 minutes.

SOUPS

Beef Stew

Black Bean Soup

Cheesy Bean Soup

Cheesy Potato and Ham Soup

Cheesy Vegetable Soup

Chicken and Vegetable Chowder

Chicken Noodle Soup

Chicken Noodle Stew

Chicken Stew

Chicken Vegetable Soup

Easy Clam Chowder

Easy Potato Soup

Ham and Potato Soup

Oyster Stew

Peanut Soup

Southwest Chicken Fiesta

Southwest Potato Soup

Southwestern Stew

Taco Soup

Vegetable Beef Soup

BEEF STEW

1 16 oz can roast beef in gravy

1 soup can water

1 can crinkle cut carrots, drained

2 to 3 tablespoons instant potato flakes

1 can beef gravy

2 cans whole potatoes, drained and cubed

salt and pepper to taste

Combine the beef chunks, gravy, water, cubed potatoes, and carrots in a slow cooker. Cook on low for 4 to 6 hours or on high 2 hours. Taste and use salt and pepper if needed. If the broth is thinner than you like, stir the instant potato flakes into ½ cup of the hot gravy and add back to the slow cooker to thicken. Cook for an additional ½ hour if the potato flakes are added.

NOTE: This may be cooked on the stove. Bring to a near boil and simmer for 20 minutes. Check the seasoning and thickness and add the potato flakes if desired.

BLACK BEAN SOUP

½ cup chopped onion

2 teaspoons garlic powder

2 cans black beans, rinsed and drained

1 pouch chicken breast

1 tablespoon lime juice

1 tablespoon oil

1 can chicken broth

½ cup salsa

1 cup cooked rice

1 teaspoon cumin

Sauté the onion in the oil until tender. Combine all ingredients in a slow cooker and cook on low for 6 to 8 hours or on high for 4 hours.

NOTE: This may be cooked on the stove. Bring to a near boil and simmer for 20 minutes.

CHEESY BEER SOUP

½ cup chopped onion

1 16 oz box of processed cheese food, cubed

½ cup beer

6 precooked bacon slices, chopped

1 tablespoon oil

1 can chicken broth

½ teaspoon Worcestershire sauce

Sauté the onion in the oil until tender. Add the cheese, broth, and Worcestershire sauce. Stir constantly on low heat until the cheese is melted, approximately 5 minutes. Stir in the beer. Sprinkle with the chopped bacon for garnish when serving.

CHEESY POTATO AND HAM SOUP

2 tablespoons butter
¼ cup minced canned ham
1 soup can milk made from dry

¼ cup chopped onion
1 can cream of potato soup
1 cup Cheddar cheese

Mix all ingredients and bring to a near boil. Simmer for 10 minutes.

NOTE: Chopped precooked bacon or chopped country ham from commercially vacuum sealed package may be used instead of the canned ham.

CHEESY VEGETABLE SOUP

1 can cream style corn
½ cup canned carrot slices, drained
½ cup chopped onion
2 cans chicken broth

1 can whole potatoes, drained
½ cup canned green beans, drained
½ teaspoon pepper
1 ½ cups grated Cheddar cheese

Combine all ingredients except the cheese in a slow cooker and cook on low for 4 to 6 hours or on high for 3 hours. Stir in the cheese and cook on low for another ½ hour until the cheese is melted.

NOTE: This may also be cooked on the stove. Bring to a near boil and simmer for 10 minutes. Stir in the cheese and simmer for an additional 10 minutes until the cheese is melted.

CHICKEN AND VEGETABLE CHOWDER

¼ cup chopped onion
2 tablespoons flour
2 teaspoons chicken bouillon granules
1 pouch chicken breast
4 slices precooked bacon, diced

2 tablespoon butter
2 cups water
2 cups milk made from dry
1 can mixed vegetables, drained

Sauté the onion in the butter for 2 minutes until tender. Remove the onion and whisk the flour into the butter. Dissolve the bouillon in the water and slowly add to the flour mixture, whisking until smooth. Cook over medium heat for 5 minutes. Stir in the milk and heat for 3 minutes. Do not boil. Add the chicken and the vegetables and heat for 3 minutes. Do not boil. Top each bowl of chowder with the diced bacon.

NOTE: Canned chopped bacon pieces may be substituted for the precooked bacon.

CHICKEN NOODLE SOUP

3 tablespoons chicken base

1 can crinkle cut carrots, drained

1 teaspoon dried chives

1 pouch chicken breast

6 cups water

1 ½ cups dry noodles

½ teaspoon garlic powder

Dissolve the chicken base in the water and bring to a boil. Add the remaining ingredients, bring back to a boil. Reduce the heat to medium and cook 15 more minutes until the noodles are done.

NOTE: Chicken base is found beside the chicken bouillon in the store. It makes a rich, well flavored base for soups.

CHICKEN NOODLE STEW

¼ cup of butter

4 cups water

1 tablespoon dried minced onion

½ teaspoon garlic powder

1 13 oz can chicken breast

¼ cup of all purpose flour

2 teaspoons chicken bouillon granules

1 tablespoon dried chives

1 ½ cups uncooked noodles

1 can mixed vegetables, drained

Cook the noodles as directed on the package. Melt the butter and whisk in the flour until smooth. Stir in the water and whisk until smooth. Add the spices and simmer, stirring frequently, for 5 minutes until it begins to thicken. Stir in the chicken, vegetables, and the noodles and simmer for 5 more minutes until heated through.

CHICKEN STEW

2 pouches chicken chunks

½ soup can of water

1 can whole potatoes, drained and cubed

1 can cream of chicken soup

1 can mixed vegetables, drained

Mix all ingredients in a slow cooker and cook on low for 4 to 6 hours or on high for 2 hours.

NOTE: This may also be cooked on the stove. Bring to a near boil and simmer for 20 minutes.
NOTE: Canned chicken may be substituted for the chicken pouches. Add it the last 10 minutes cooking on the stove or the last hour of cooking in the slow cooker.

CHCIKEN VEGETABLE SOUP

3 tablespoons chicken base
1 can of peas and carrots, drained
1 4 oz can sliced mushrooms, drained
1 teaspoon dried chives
2 pouches chicken breast

6 cups water
½ cup baby corn, drained
1 can whole potatoes, drained
½ teaspoon garlic powder
½ teaspoon pepper

Dissolve the chicken base in the water and bring to a boil. Break the baby corn into ½" pieces. Cube the potatoes. Add the remaining ingredients and bring back to a boil. Reduce the heat to medium and cook 10 more minutes.

EASY CLAM CHOWDER

1 can cream of chicken soup
2 cans minced clams, drained
4 slices precooked bacon, chopped

1 can cream of potato soup
1 soup can water

Combine the soups, clams, and water. Bring to a near boil and simmer for 20 minutes. Top with the chopped bacon when serving.

EASY POTATO SOUP

2 cans whole potatoes, drained
2 tablespoons butter
1 can cream of celery soup
1 teaspoon dried chives

½ cup chopped onion
1 can cream of chicken soup
1 cup milk made from dry
Salt, pepper to taste

Dice the potatoes. Sauté the onion in the butter for 2 minutes until tender. Mix all ingredients and cook on medium heat until bubbly.

HAM AND POTATO SOUP

1 can cream of chicken soup
3 cups milk made from dry
2 cups canned ham
1 cup grated Cheddar cheese

1 can cream of mushroom soup
1 can whole potatoes
salt, pepper to taste

Cut the ham and the potatoes into ½" cubes. Add the soups, milk, salt, and pepper. Cook over medium heat 10 minutes, stirring frequently. Do not boil. Stir in the cheese and cook until melted.

OYSTER STEW

½ cup chopped onion
1 can cream of mushroom soup
1 teaspoon Worcestershire sauce
Salt, pepper to taste
Bacon bits to garnish

2 tablespoons butter
1 cup evaporated milk
1 can oysters, drained
1 teaspoon dried chives

Sauté the onion in the butter for 2 minutes until tender. Chop the oysters into bite sized pieces. Stir in the soup, milk, seasonings, and oysters and heat just to the boiling point but do not boil. Garnish each bowl of the stew with ½ teaspoon of the bacon bits.

PEANUT SOUP

½ cup chopped onion
1 tablespoon flour
6 tablespoons creamy peanut butter
1 teaspoon Worcestershire sauce
½ teaspoon pepper

1 tablespoon oil
2 cans chicken broth
½ cup evaporated milk
1 chicken bouillon cube
1 teaspoon hot sauce

Sauté the onion in the oil for 2 minutes until tender. Stir in the flour and mix thoroughly. Stir in the chicken broth and the remaining ingredients. Bring to a near boil, reduce the heat and simmer for 15 minutes. Season with pepper and hot sauce to taste before serving.

SOUTHWEST CHICKEN FIESTA

1 can chicken broth

1 can tomatoes with chilies

1 can black beans, rinsed and drained

½ teaspoon cumin

1 can diced tomatoes

1 pouch chicken chunks

1 cup grated Cheddar cheese

1 to 2 teaspoons chili powder

Combine all ingredients except the cheese and bring to a near boil. Reduce the heat and simmer for 20 minutes. Add the cheese and simmer until melted.

SOUTHWEST POTATO SOUP

1 5 ¼ oz box au gratin potatoes

1 can tomatoes with chilies

2 cups milk made from dry

¼ cup salsa

1 can corn, drained

2 cups water

8 oz processed cheese food, cubed

Combine the dry potatoes, the sauce mix from the box, the corn, tomatoes, water, milk, and salsa. Bring to a near boil. Reduce the heat and simmer for 20 minutes. Add the cheese and simmer until melted.

NOTE: A pouch or a small can of chicken may be added.

SOUTHWESTERN STEW

1 cup chopped onion

1 16 oz can beef in gravy

2 cans beef broth

4 teaspoons chili powder

½ teaspoon ground red pepper

1 tablespoon oil

2 cans Mexican style tomatoes

1 6 oz can tomato paste

1 tablespoon Italian seasoning

¼ teaspoon cinnamon

Sauté the onion in the oil for 2 minutes until tender. Combine all ingredients in a slow cooker and cook on low for 6 to 8 hours or on high for 4 hours.

NOTE: Regular diced tomatoes may be substituted for the Mexican style tomatoes.

TACO SOUP

1 can kidney beans
1 can black beans
1 can chopped green chilies
½ cup finely chopped onion

1 can whole kernel corn
1 can stewed tomatoes
1 envelope taco seasoning mix
1 16 oz can tomato sauce

Mix all ingredients in a slow cooker. Cook on low for 5 hours or on high for 3 hours.

NOTE: See Appetizers for Taco Dip.

VEGETABLE BEEF SOUP

1 16 ox can beef in gravy
1 to 2 cans diced tomatoes
1 can whole potatoes, drained and cubed
½ can cut baby corn or ½ cup canned corn, drained

1 can beef gravy
1 can green beans, drained
1 can crinkle cut carrots, drained
1 4 oz can sliced mushrooms, drained

Combine all the ingredients in a slow cooker. Depending on the thickness you want, use either 1 or both cans of the diced tomatoes. Cook on low for 6 to 8 hours or on high for 4 hours.

NOTE: This may be cooked on the stove. Bring to a near boil and simmer for 20 minutes.

APPETIZERS

Bean and Bacon Dip	2
BBQ Chicken in Cornbread Cups	2
Cheese Fondue	2
Chicken Nests	3
Crab Nests	3
Devilled Eggs	4
Fried Onion Rings	4
Ham Bites	4
Ham Nests	5
Hot Artichoke Dip	5
Marinated Cheese Cubes	6
Marinated Mushrooms	6
Mini Ham Quiches	6
Pickled Eggs and Beets	7
Pineapple Salsa	7
Rosy Pickled Eggs	7
Shrimp and Pineapple Appetizers	8
Spiced Pecans	8
Spiced Walnuts	8
Stuffed Pickles	9
Taco Dip	9
Texas Caviar	9
Tuna Curry	10
Very Cheesy Chili Dip	10

BEVERAGES

Chocolate Mocha Mix	12
Cranberry and Grapefruit Juice	12
Cranberry Punch	12
Eggless Eggnog	12
Hot Chocolate Mix	13
Hot Spiced "Cider"	13
Lime Water	13
Mexican Coffee	13
Minted Chocolate Mocha Mix	14
Spiced Tea Mix	14
Spicy Tomato Juice	14
White Grape Tea	15

BREADS

Batter Bread	18
Beer Bread	18
Cheese Straws	18
Cheese Wafers	18
Cheesy Onion Bread	19
Corn Cakes	19
Cornbread Cups	20
Crispy Cheese Crackers	20
Crispy Tortilla Chips	20
Dumplings	20
Easy Corn Cakes	21
Easy Spoon Rolls	21
Flour Tortillas	21
Lime Muffins	22
Mexican Corn Bread	22
No Knead Cheese Bread	22
Oat Batter Bread	23
Pizza Crust	23
Potato Bread	23
Pumpkin Slow Cooker Bread	24
Quick Cheese and Pepper Bread	24
Simple White Bread	24
Stir and Roll Pizza Crust	25
Tortilla Shells	25

BREAKFASTS

Applesauce Muffins	28
Bacon and Eggs	28

CHICKEN

COOKIES

DESSERTS

HAMS (Canned & Country)

MEATLESS ENTREES

3262154

Made in the USA